Licia Iverson and Tom Massey watch author sign book contract.

There is some great material here and the potential for a highly popular book. I found it to be fun reading, insightful, and provocative, with vivid descriptions of how to do a number of things we never had the nerve to try. I really liked the format — the short narrative chapters, each accompanied by a succinct moral point, make for easy access and delivery of a poignant message.

With hobo royalty — Minneapolis Jewel and King Tuck

I started reading *Hobo Sapien*. I like the way it's written — a different take on the various freight train hopping books and articles that I have read. I am enjoying it.

— Minneapolis Jewel, three-time national Hobo Queen
at the annual Britt, Iowa Hobo Convention

HOBO
SAPIEN

FREIGHT TRAIN HOPPING TAO AND ZEN

WAYNE IVERSON

Robert D. Reed Publishers   •   Bandon, OR 97411

Robert D. Reed Publishers
P.O. Box 1992
Bandon, OR 97411
Phone: 541-347-9882; Fax: -9883
E-mail: 4bobreed@msn.com
Website: www.rdrpublishers.com

Editors: Pat Conway and Melynda Saldenais
Front Cover Art: Erik C. Lindgren
Cover Designer: Cleone L. Reed
Photographer: Tom Lee
Book Designer: Debby Gwaltney

FSC
Mixed Sources
Product group from well-managed
forests and other controlled sources
Cert no. SW-COC-002283
www.fsc.org
© 1996 Forest Stewardship Council

ISBN 13: 978-1-934759-43-1
ISBN 10: 1-934759-43-0

Library of Congress Control Number: 2010928001

Manufactured, Typeset, and Printed in the United States of America

Wayne   Ron   Jim

Dedicated to my brother, Jim Iverson,
who *caught the westbound* in 1961

🚂 ACKNOWLEDGMENTS 🚃

Meister Eckhart said, "If the only prayer you said in your whole life was, 'thank you,' that would suffice." I have a lot of people to thank — most importantly my wife, Licia. Thank you for being a strong, independent woman who is my equal. Thank you for the countless ways you supported me in this process. Licia and I met on Mother's Day 1992 at a party hosted by the Petty's in Evergreen, Colorado and had "his" and "hers" weddings in 1994. The rest is history, social studies, biology, and home economics. Standing four-feet, nine-inches in her high-heel sneakers, this child development genius was once asked by one of her four-year old students if she had been put in the dryer. In addition, my parents, Margaret and Stan, also deserve gold medals for enduring my vagabond ways.

Pastor Mark Heiss of the Park City Community Church in Utah was immensely supportive during my stint there. When he hired me to teach meditation, he also asked me to preach periodically. In my first talk in December 1990, I included a well-received freight train hopping tale that has since become the chapter titled "Trains and Transcendence." The freight train parable was born. A rejected *Park City Magazine* piece became "A Real Trooper." Editor Keith Arum of the *Park City E.A.R.* was kind enough to write an article about me called "Hobo Sapien: A Tall Man's Tales of Zen and the Art of Hobo," as well as award me third prize in his writing contest for "Cinder Dicks."

Significant progress on the book occurred when my wife and I moved to Glenwood Springs, Colorado in 1997. On September 9, 1999, Karen Chamberlain and Carol Bell formed an exceptional writer's group, which I attended regularly. Pat Conway was a founding member of the group, took over as co-leader when Carol moved away, and also helped edit the book. The Aspen Writer's Group was also helpful. In November 2000, I provided security on a film shot in Aspen called *Winter Break*, where I worked with Sarah George, director of the freight train hopping documentary *Catching Out*. I wrote extensively while guarding the sets and equipment overnight. Al Lyons of Aspen Stage produced a radio version of "Cinder Dicks" for the *Aspen Leaves in the Air* show. He also put my children's story "The Wishbone" on the air, performed my comedy *Tenitis* at the *Five-Minute Play Festival*, and directed a glorified staged reading of my drama *Chasing Messiahs*.

After we moved to Oklahoma in 2001, a wonderful writing instructor named Mel Odom gave me an assignment to write a "how to hop a freight train" magazine article. It was published in 2004 (with substantial unapproved changes) and has now morphed into the chapter titled "Yuppie See, Yuppie Do." Also in 2004, I went on a Lutz-led river rafting trip through Desolation Canyon on the Green River in Utah. I gave a draft of *Hobo Sapien* to fellow floater Chris Valenti, who passed it on to his stepmother, Susan Vogel of Pince-Nez Press. Susan became my muse for two years.

Sue Cruz, Geoff Delin, R. S. Fabrick, and John Perry gave the manuscript a thorough examination from a spiritual perspective. Andy Horton of the University of Oklahoma (OU) Film and Video Studies program provided valuable advice and got me an audience with OU Press. Thurman White, whose biography I wrote, encouraged me to enter a master's degree program he helped create at the University of Oklahoma. My superb advisor, Sue Schofield, connected me with Professor Tom Boyd, who critiqued the book and wrote its foreword. Curt Coy was my trusty sidekick on the hop out of Gainsville, Texas, which is chronicled in Chapters 37 and 38. Phil and Leigh Vincent from Sooner Copy Center in Norman, Oklahoma provided splendid services.

I put the book on the shelf for two years while I worked on a detailed step outline and back-stories for either a television series or trilogy of films. Then while I was working in Colorado in the winter of 2009, Tom Massey, who had read an earlier draft of this missive in 2001, told my wife to have me contact him when I returned to Oklahoma. He offered to send my book to his publisher with a strong recommendation. Bob and Cleone Reed were kind enough to pick up the title.

When I began communicating with the Reeds, my wife was on vacation in Bandon, Oregon with her sister. Her maiden name just happens to be Reid (close enough for Deity work). Bandon is the location of Robert D. Reed Publishers. When I mentioned that I was driving buses in Alaska, Cleone asked whether or not I knew the husband of one of her best friends who drove buses in Denali National Park. Mark was living two doors down from me in the dormitory. Bob signed the book contract on 9/9/09 (at 9:09 p.m.), exactly ten years after the founding of the Glenwood Springs writer's group that was so instrumental in its creation. Also that fall, Tom Boyd successfully used *Hobo Sapien* in his Religious Studies class called "Religion, Culture and the Meaning of Life." His summary of the experience and student comments about the book are on page 122.

In the spirit of train tales with spiritual twists, artwork and photographs of hatha yoga poses done on freight train cars are included. Erik Lindgren did the stunning cover art. Tom Lee took several wonderful photographs. Melynda Saldenais zealously edited the final draft. There is more information about these friends on page 119.

I am a disciple of Paramahansa Yogananda and endeavor to follow his teachings. If I have not in this book, the fault lies with me alone. I am a member of his Self-Realization Fellowship organization, but I do not represent it.

Wayne Iverson
Norman, Oklahoma

🚂 TABLE OF CONTENTS 🚂

PHOTOGRAPHS

There are photographs on pages 1, 2, 5, 13, 24, 25, 26, 27, 60, 61, 84, 85, 107, 120, and 127.

Hobo Sapien: A New Find in the Evolution of a Species

When I hear the distant wail of a train whistle in the deep of the night, I am immediately elsewhere. It evokes that boundless realm where *possibility* beckons. This feeling has its origin in early childhood when my father worked for the railroad and we lived quite close to tracks. The same moans evoked images of what might be, mediated through the stories told at family gatherings.

When I read Wayne Iverson's manuscript, *Hobo Sapien*, that same mood stirred afresh. It became extended much further, as I realized that those trains of my childhood were bound to have borne in them clandestine riders, unknown to me, to the railroad management, to the *bulls*. They were actually living the possibilities that only occupied my child's fantasy.

The title itself is sufficient to compel attention. Only one letter separates it from the previous stage of evolution beyond which we so desperately need to evolve. But "hobo?" Iverson uses his forty chapters to release the hobo from encrusted images that keep him (her?) imbedded in stereotypes of the irregular, the unorthodox way of life. He does more than "humanize" the hobo. He renders an all-American but counter-image of a free human being, and he does so by unveiling the spiritual depths, which can hardly be encountered without the spirit of the hobo sapien.

Iverson's clever way of achieving this end lies in his multidimensional story. It takes place in four interlaced and intimately related accounts. First, this story is autobiographical, but very oddly so. While Iverson tells his story, taking us on a whirlwind adventure across the American West, the book is not *about* his story. He is a mediator of something that comes through him but does not derive from him. We learn almost nothing of his childhood, his family, or his "official" career. He comes on the scene as a young man, intent on escaping academia — Yale University, no less — and plotting a novel personal course. He becomes a joyful *outsider*, who, as Colin Wilson once put it, "sees too much and too deep" to remain on the inside. He only flirts with established life, as if playing in someone else's yard and using his water hose. For all of his self-referential presentation, Iverson remains mysteriously elusive in and through his story. On the one hand, we learn much about him as a hobo and as a mystic in the making. On the other hand, he remains ephemeral to our sense of what an American male of his age and kind should be. He's playing with us and asking us to play.

Second, this story is a history, but for those who do not appreciate history, do not be alarmed. It is anything but a stuffy recitation of chronological events or their interpretation. The sequence of events is present but only barely. One might even call the history most nearly *impressionist*. Yes, there are dates, personalities, events, but they arise in the milieu of the lived experience of one voice. Iverson pauses, as it were, to allow the reader to sense the larger tapestry of time in which his experience is imbedded.

And what history is this? It is a history of the American West as seen through the imprint of railroads upon it. Every town and the varied landscape west of the Mississippi is tied together, geographically and sequentially, by the power of rails. The fact of the train becomes an implicit metaphor of connection between otherwise disparate towns, communities and regions scattered through the Rockies and beyond in all directions. Not everything is said that could be said about how the railroad defined this domain, nor need it be said. What is said is enough to grasp the connection of human engagement in time and space and the way railroads threaded the connection.

Third, this is a story about hobos. Of course, Iverson *is* a hobo, and we see the "type" made visible through him. But his interest is not in making himself the archetypal hobo. In fact, he is not the archetype, only a peculiar version of it: a part-time hobo. His interest lies in allowing the spirit of the hobo to reveal itself through his travels and the array of humanity he meets along the way. Not everyone he meets is a hobo, but he places each person within the human ferment and reveals their complex and shadowy character. He brings them from the shadows and introduces them to us, through himself. He makes us long to be a hobo, if only in the deep of the night when listening to the low moan of a train whistle. Hobos become us, only discerned from another side, the side we tuck away in interior worlds we imagine as we drive to work and back home to appear, above all, *normal*. But what are the norms and how do we recognize "normal" amid the endless diversity of the human species?

Finally, and most to the point in *Hobo Sapien*, this is the story of a spiritual life and the pilgrimage involved. Iverson's sojourn is grounded in another dimension, quite beyond the constraints of time, space, embodiment and personality. He is on a journey beyond self into soul and beyond that into the All. Drawing largely, but not exclusively, on Eastern teachings, symbols, and practices, he invites us to see what he and the hobo knows: that all of the so-called "best laid plans of mice and men" are more nearly snares than means to the liberation of our kind. Liberation comes by letting go of place and our status in it and entering the space to which we are most closely allied, even if we utterly deny and ignore it. It is the space of Being Itself, what we commonly call the God Space.

Once again, if this language proves troubling, do not be alarmed. Iverson walks softly through the verbiage of devotion to the mystical Oneness. He, like all effective teachers, only points. He leaves the rest to us. He invites, but only through the witness he offers of a way of living that finds its home in the depths of our very being, not in anything we can or need to master, manage or control. It is as though he is suggesting on every page that we ride the rails of inwardness on its multiple-lifetime journey into destiny. He seeks to say nothing new in all of this, but only strives to uncover the perennial and universal way that we can discover by joining him as spiritual hobos.

The book echoes the same general timbre as *Zen and the Art of Motorcycle Maintenance*. Persig's work is three-dimensional, but Iverson's has four levels. While Iverson does not present the "spiritual rationality" that Persig offers, he does both inform and inspire reflective response.

This is a good book, not only because of its multidimensional yet unified presentation, but because it is genuinely a funny book. There are actual jokes along the way, but they slip in at just the juncture where we suspect that the author may be about to "go serious" on us. Beyond the jokes, however, lies the wit. It rests in that playfulness which marks the writing of a liberated writer. Ah yes, a hobo writer. Read it and enjoy… or be disturbed… or be transformed.

Tom W. Boyd
University of Oklahoma

After teaching philosophy at the University of Oklahoma for twenty-eight years, Tom W. Boyd retired from full time teaching in 1997. He also retired from the ordained ministry in the Presbyterian Church USA in 1998. Tom continues to teach in the newly established Religious Studies program of the university and to lecture, preach, conduct seminars, and write. Tom holds four earned degrees, including a Ph.D. in Religion from Vanderbilt University. His academic specialization is in philosophical theology, philosophy of religion and ethics. His current concentration is on the relation among world religions and the relation between religion and culture.

Photo by Tom Lee

In June 2006, CNN reported that a man had just called 911 on his cell phone from a freight yard in Texas to report that a train had severed his legs. DO NOT HOP FREIGHT TRAINS! It's illegal. It's rough. It's dangerous. You could wake up dead. I don't normally advocate living life vicariously, but I do when it comes to *catching out* or *riding the rails* as the hobos refer to it.

People become hobos for many reasons: wanderlust, economic hardship, Post-Traumatic Stress Syndrome, and plain old anarchy, which played a role in the Wobbly past and is a major reason younger riders, who prefer to be called tramps, hop today. A hobo named Doc just had hard luck. In Michael Mathers' *Riding the Rails*, Doc says, "I joined the lonely hearts club one time . . . and sent my picture to it and they sent it back to me. Said they wasn't that lonely."

People have been taking free rides on freight trains since the Civil War. Many did it to work on distant farms. Some brought their own hoes along. They became known as "hoe boys." Say that with a Southern drawl (especially after some Southern Comfort) and presto, a new word is added to the dictionary — hobo. Edward Hays suggests another derivation in *A Lenten Hobo Honeymoon*. He claims that the word "hooboo" was a Negro slave term that eventually morphed to become part of white working-class jargon. Many slaves were sent to America from Africa's Gambia River basin. In West African folk tradition, a hooboo was a ghost condemned to constantly wander the country dressed in rags, depending on strangers for food. To this day, in that region, it is considered good fortune to help any poor wandering person.

I am such a poor wandering person, "poor in spirit" anyway. As mentioned in the Beatitudes of Jesus, to be "poor in spirit" means to gradually reduce our attachment to earthly possessions, materially minded friends, and selfish human love in order to focus more strongly on our inner being. Both hobos and mystics lessen their material desires, but mystics do it so they can focus more on their souls. The hobo may be an icon of freedom, but it can be freedom without responsibility — doing what we want to do when we want to do it. Most people have responsibility without freedom — doing what we're taught to do when we're taught to do it. What I advocate is moving to the mystic depths that all the higher religions possess. That is true freedom, freedom with responsibility — doing what we ought to do when we ought to do it. That is also wisdom. *Hobo sapien* means wise hobo. Be a *hobo sapien*.

My definition of a mystic is someone who meditates daily and actually experiences God to some degree. Anthony de Mello tells a story about a king in India who wanted to know God. He called in a holy man and said,

"I'm very busy, tell me how to find God in one sentence."
The holy man laughed and said, "I can do so in one word."
"What is that word?"
"Silence."
"And how do I achieve silence?"
"Meditation."
"And what is meditation?"
"Silence."

Father Thomas Keating, who is reviving long-lost Christian meditation methods through his Contemplative Outreach organization, said, "Silence is God's first language, everything else is a poor translation." In the Old Testament's Book of Ecclesiastes it says, "Better a handful of quietness than two handfuls of toil and striving after wind." Mose Allison described the state of most people when he penned the lyrics, "If silence was golden, you couldn't raise a dime." Be still and know.

This book is a series of stand-alone freight train parables, tales of my hoboing adventures with a moral. This is in the hobo tradition. Some hobos stay in missions. Some missions require residents to listen to a sermon before they can get food or bed. You have to listen to my pithy ranting to get into the hobo underworld. I do inject my twisted brand of humor to help the medicine go down. Sleeping through mission sermons is also traditional, so by skipping each chapter's last paragraph you can usually ignore the lessons and wait for a jolt from the Cosmic Chattel Prod.

Hobo Sapien is modeled structurally on the *Tao Te Ching*. The *Tao* is only eighty-one chapters and eighty-one pages long, yet it has more to say than most tomes. I cannot match its spiritual brilliance, but I did try to match its simplicity. To paraphrase the *Tao*, "Those who write do not know; those who know do not write." At least I've tried to limit my not knowing. The chapters are organized chronologically by the date of the freight train hops. The first chapter of the book is a chronology of my life so you can refer back to it if you get confused. But as my friend Mark observed, the format fits the topic. A book on freight train riding should hop around a bit. If it's jarring, so is a ride in a boxcar.

Chit is the Sanskrit word for "pure consciousness." If you purchased this missive at a book signing you probably received a bookmark that reads, "CHIT HAPPENS." Use it to mark your place, and when you are done, tape it to your mirror, stick it on your bumper, put it in your window, or paste it on your husband's forehead as a reminder to keep raising consciousness. Let's kick that other saying in the "S."

🚂 CHAPTER 1: DRAPETOMANIA 🚂

A Depression-era hobo named Connecticut Slim once claimed that there was a medical term for wanderlust: drapetomania. I contracted it. During my freshman year at Yale in 1967, I took a religious studies class that blew out the cornerstone of my fundamentalist beliefs. My dogma got run over by my karma. Then the correlation principle set in. It states that a change in one thing produces changes in everything else. I began to question my entire direction in life. Yale is not a good place to go through an identity crisis. I left college with a friend in 1969 and eventually transitioned from "Yale to rail."

Our adventures began immediately. We hitched a ride in a stolen car to Florida. There I became friends with a character named Jerry, who often told me that my mother should have pinched off my head and sold the milk. Jerry and I left Florida in the spring of 1969 in his Plymouth Deathtrap. It died and Jerry gave it to a junk dealer for a ride to the bus depot. We took the Greyhound to Nebraska and did construction work. Then we were employed at Don's Bar in Memphis, Nebraska. I had a previous obligation in Minnesota that summer, so Don arranged a ride for me in a hearse taking a body to Iowa for internment (deadheading). I hitchhiked the rest of the way.

I got trapped in Minnesota. I bought an El Camino truck and a Honda 750 motorcycle. I thought they would bring me freedom. Instead, they made me an indentured servant. I had to work constantly to make payments. The Hindus say, "He who has cow has care of cow." They are correct. I compared the simplicity of hitchhiking with the entrapment of possessions and shed a few, but it was almost two years until my drapetomania was assuaged again during my *Then Came Bronson* period.

Bronson was a TV show about a young newspaperman who set out on a cross-country trip on his Harley in a quest for the meaning of life. I sold the El Camino and rode a November cold front on my Honda down to Phoenix, Arizona for winter warmth. A recent viewing of the movie *Easy Rider* kept me nervously on the lookout for pickup trucks with gun racks. I suffered poverty in Arizona. But that forced simplicity led to a mystic experience. I spent a composure-stretching evening bar hopping with the state's biggest outlaw motorcycle pack — and lived to brag about it.

The next spring, I joaded to California. A Chinese gang stole my motorcycle in San Francisco. I returned to Minnesota to work construction, went to Europe, and returned to Yale in 1972 eager to learn. But Yale and I had grown in opposite directions. My semester there still ranks as the most depressing time of my life. I looked into experimental schools across the country and The Evergreen State College in Olympia, Washington was the best and the cheapest. I transferred there. After nearly two years, I finally got my motorcycle back and sold it to pay tuition in 1973. I didn't own another vehicle for over twenty years. I began to hop freight trains, but trespassed responsibly and left no trace of my activities. A verse in Woody Guthrie's song "This Land is Your Land" goes, "And that sign said 'no tresspassin.' But on the other side it didn't say nothin! Now that side was made for you and me!"

Though Evergreen was a perfect fit, I couldn't attend for more than two quarters in a row without a reality check — like raising tomatoes in the Smoky Mountains of Tennessee. After graduation in 1975, I lived in ski resort towns Park City, Utah, Brian Head, Utah and Telluride, Colorado doing city planning, drinking excessively and womanizing. After losing a Telluride City Council election by one vote in 1981, I returned to Minnesota for two years and got serious about spirituality. I went monastic in California for seven years. I lived in Los Angeles for a record four years. Those four years also represent my longest job tenure — in the monastery print shop.

After my stint as a monk, I lived in Park City again for three years working part-time as a pastoral assistant and a water master. Later, even living in ideal places like Evergreen, Colorado after I married, I still got the itch to move every four years. My wife likes to nest. In 2001, I easily convinced Licia to move to Norman, Oklahoma — to help her aged parents. During this time, I cared for other elders in their homes as well. We lived there nine years. Working summers in Alaska and returning to freight train hopping kept drapetomania at bay. I barely work within the system. I don't stay at a job long, but few regret hiring me. I have certainly checked out of the materialistic mainstream. Our car's only bumper sticker quotes Gandhi, "Live Simply So That Others May Simply Live."

I never experienced *hobo jungles*. Freight train hopping was my major mode of transportation, but not my lifestyle. I stayed in two missions, but I usually had places to go and people to see. I used to think that financial necessity should be a criterion for hopping trains and criticized yuppie hobos. But necessity can take non-economic forms, too. My Colorado friend, Pat Conway, wrote in the column of one of my chapters, "I think the highest spiritual attainment is a total release of the need to judge." Non-judging is most likely a side effect of the highest spiritual attainment, and it still eludes my grasp.

Freedom from wanderlust, whether the freight train or cruise ship type, only comes from contacting the soul. The soul is made in God's image; hence one of its characteristics is omnipresence. A little travel is fine, but venturing to faraway places is a poor substitute for the "everywhereness" that is our birthright. Thomas Merton said that the fastest way to get to God is to go to our own center and pass through that center into the center of God. It is that centering — not traveling — that provides the antidote for drapetomania. The Kingdom of Heaven is within you.

The sixties really happened in the seventies. Were it possible to graph the number of people hitchhiking during that time, the results would have given a good indication of overall hippie activity. By 1973, there were so many people "thumbing" that on some freeway entrance ramps, you almost had to take a number and wait your turn. There could be seven or more people in a row waiting for a ride. I don't do lines well. I decided to *catch out*.

I had finished the school year at The Evergreen State College and had construction work lined up in Minnesota for the summer. En route to Minneapolis, I rode to Spokane, Washington with some friends from college. I had a map of the major rail lines in the country copied from a library atlas. The day before I departed, I looked up the address of the Burlington Northern Railroad yard in the Yellow Pages. My friend, Cindy, drove me there. A yardman told me that a train left for Minneapolis every day around noon. When Cindy brought me back at eleven o'clock the next morning, my train was already pulling out. Schedules aren't a railroad priority, although "early" is a rarity. I ran up to a passing flatcar and high jumped onto it like I was in a track meet — damaging my knee slightly in the process. I waved enthusiastically to the men I soon passed in the nearby *hobo jungle*. They didn't wave back. My eagerness betrayed me as a greenhorn (they called them *gay-cats* in the nineteenth century). It wasn't pretty, but that was the start of twelve years of serious, steady freight train riding.

I was on the old Great Northern Railway's Hi-Line route. The railroad was the brainchild of "The Empire Builder," Canadian-born James J. Hill. He allegedly said, "Give me snuff, whiskey, and Swedes, and I will build a railroad to hell." Hill started out as an agent for the old St. Paul and Pacific Railroad (SP&P) in 1866. With other Canadian investors, he purchased the company in 1879 and vastly expanded it. Hill reorganized the SP&P into the Great Northern Railroad (GN) and set out in 1889 to become the first person to build a transcontinental railroad without public money or land grants. Completed in 1893, the GN was the only transcontinental railroad that did not go bankrupt. Hill later absorbed the Northern Pacific Railroad in 1896 and tried to do likewise with the Chicago, Burlington, and Quincy Railroad. Bullets prevented it. President William McKinley was assassinated in 1901 and trust-busting Teddy Roosevelt and the Supreme Court stopped him.

It took three days to get to Minneapolis on that first jaunt. During a layover in Minot, North Dakota, I saw two women *catching out* together. I've never seen any since, but I know they're out there — hopefully riding in pairs for safety. Three days on a freight train was brutal. I never rode that long again. Instead of replacing hitchhiking (begging) with freight train riding (taking), I ended up melding the two — thumbing through the states that were easy on hitchers and hopping in the states that weren't.

I thought my rail-riding career ended in November 1984 when I joined the monastic order of the Self-Realization Fellowship in California. I knew the answer I would receive if I asked my superiors for permission to use that particular mode of transportation. Under a vow of obedience, I gave up hoboing. When I left the order several years later, I preached occasionally in Methodist and Unity churches, where I developed the freight train homily or parable. I told tales from my hobo days and gave them spiritual twists. I entered one of them in a writing contest in a Utah newspaper. It won third prize. The editor said it was by far the best story, but the writing was terrible. Like a hobo running alongside a moving boxcar, my writing is starting to catch up with the quality of my stories.

I married in 1994 and we bought the first car I'd owned in over twenty years. For once when I heard that lonesome whistle, I was called to write, not to ride. Then I hopped a train in the summer of 1997 from Glenwood Springs, Colorado to Grand Junction, Colorado to see what had changed in the thirteen years since I stopped riding *Old Dirty Face*. I was also seeking inspiration to write this book. Then I *caught out* in Alaska in June of 2000 just to say I had. After moving to Oklahoma and exploring every county, wanderlust struck again. I hopped four trains in 2005 and three in 2006. My mother and my wife were not overjoyed. I have now ridden freights in every state west of the Mississippi River, except for South Dakota, and in a few states east of the "Father of Waters."

You already know that I do not want you to parallel my rail riding tracks. I want you to experience God — not blindly believe or reject without scientific testing. The term "God" may make you cringe. I like it because it is only three letters long and "Ra" sounds too much like a high school cheer. God is not male or female, but both and neither. I believe that God does not punish us; we punish ourselves by misuse of our free will. These ideas may make you uncomfortable or even angry.

As the great Persian poet, Hafiz, writes,

> "Pulling out the chair
> Beneath your mind
> And watching you fall upon God –
> What else is there
> For Hafiz to do
> That is any fun in this world?"

What else is there for me to do, too?

Murder. Twice. That was why my freight train riding companion, Jimbo, had done two stints in prison. He'd just broken parole and his attorney told him that his best defense was to get the hell out of California and never come back.

I met Jimbo when I was hitchhiking from San Francisco to Phoenix in April 1974. One of my rides took me to Bakersfield, California, where I was dropped off next to the Southern Pacific Railroad yards. (It was in the famous U. S. Supreme Court case of Santa Clara County v. Southern Pacific Railroad where Court Reporter Bancroft Davis, the former president of the Newburgh and New York Railway, ruled in his headnotes to the case that the Fourteenth Amendment to the Constitution applied to corporations. An amendment meant to protect former slaves was twisted to make economic slaves of many Americans.) I'd never ridden trains down South, so I didn't know where they went. I spied two men under a bridge who looked like they were waiting to hop. I inquired and Jimbo said a train was coming through in about a half-hour headed for Yuma, Arizona. I decided to ride with them.

While we were waiting for the train, Jimbo told me about one of his homicides. He had gotten into a bar fight. The other guy pulled a knife. Jimbo pulled a gun and shot him. He might have made up the story, but it didn't seem prudent to say, "Oh yeah, prove you murdered him." Instead, I took out the freight train version of flight insurance. I walked over to a liquor store a few blocks away and came back with a big jug of cheap wine and some Bugler rolling tobacco. Jimbo looked at my purchase and his face lit up. He looked me in the eye and said, "Buddy, I probably can't do you any good, but I sure as hell won't do you any harm."

The ploy worked. Even if you don't drink, carry a jug with you and share it. Accept alcohol from another hobo, too, even if he has leprosy, unless you want the person to be suspicious of you. You can pretend to drink if you have to. Hobos often use *Tokay blankets*. They drink Tokay wine or other spirits until they can't feel the cold.

Jimbo didn't pretend. He got drunk very quickly. Our ride that sunny afternoon was on the back end of a grain car with a good platform. I first noticed how drunk he was when the train stopped *in the hole* — on a sidetrack. When we got off the *grainer* to relieve ourselves, Jimbo fell off the ladder and rolled down an embankment. He jumped bolt upright as if to show us he wasn't inebriated, but he struggled to get back up the ladder. When the train started moving again, he would pass out, then wake up and not remember who we were. He'd start to reach into the inside pocket of his shabby sport coat. I was afraid of that pocket's unknown contents. To stir his memory, I'd say to him in a loud voice, "JIMBO, BUDDY, DO

YOU WANT SOME MORE WINE?" His eyes would come into slow-motion focus as he gradually recognized me.

"Wayne, yer my bes fren in the whole worl."

He'd hug me, drink some more rotgut, and then pass out again. We'd go through the whole routine every thirty minutes or so. Eventually, I saw what he had in his coat pocket — an old paring knife. Still, I got tired of repeating the scene like the perpetual rehearsal of a bad play. Just as we neared the Tehachapi Loop, I climbed up on the top of the car to get away from him.

Completed in 1876, the Tehachapi Loop was one of the greatest engineering feats of its day. The Central Pacific Railroad, co-builder of the first transcontinental railroad, wanted to link their rails in Central California to those in Southern California. The rugged Tehachapi Mountains tried to stop them, as the elevation on the four-thousand foot Tehachapi Pass rose too quickly. Constructing the unique loop solved the problem. The Chinese who worked on the project called the loop "Walong" or "Coiled Dragon." With today's longer trains, the locomotives pass over the top of the end cars.

Unfortunately, Frank, the other rider, moved with me to the top of the car. He was a "Jesus freak" — the type Jim Ringer sang thusly about, "He used to take acid, and now he loves God, but he's still got that look in his eye." As we looped, he told me God's plan for my life. My intended major at Yale was religious studies. "Religious Stud" is how it showed up on my report cards. My specialty was immaculate conceptions. Needless to say, my companion couldn't foil or follow me. He magnetized our conversations on the reel of an old boom box and played them back periodically. Twice I had to listen to a circuitous conversation that I never wanted to have in the first place. I made the choice between proselyte and paring knife and climbed back down to the platform to be with the murderer.

We traversed the San Gabriel Mountains over Cajon Pass and got into San Bernardino, California late that night. I left Jimbo and Frank sleeping on the grain car and *caught out* on a different train to Yuma. I still wonder whether the Jesus freak converted Jimbo before Jimbo knifed him.

I once heard a young man accidentally mispronounce "evangelism" as "evandalism." How appropriate — it is like spray-painting your beliefs inside someone else's mind. If we make every effort to change our own life for the better our example will change others — without pestering them.

Jimbo was not the only bad boy on the block. If you are thinking of riding a freight train: 1) go to www.deadtrainbums.com and see what you will look like with your legs severed; 2) tour your local jailhouse and decide whether or not you would like to lodge there; and 3) find the toughest biker bar in town and see if you would like to hang several days with the clientele. Here are a few types of people you might encounter on freights.

Robert Silveria, Jr. is possibly the world's first serial railroad murderer. This heroin addict's alias is "Sidetrack." He had "freedom" tattooed on his neck — the "without responsibility" kind. He was dubbed "The Boxcar Killer" after he was arrested in 1996 and confessed to bludgeoning fourteen people in a spree from Florida to Montana. Sometimes he even killed his victims' dogs. Silveria usually murdered homeless transients, but his victims also included college students trying to hop freights. He usually pulled their shirts over their heads. Silveria is currently serving a double life sentence in Oregon for two of the murders. Though he claims otherwise, several police officers say he was a member of the notorious Freight Train Riders of America (FTRA).

The FTRA should not be confused with the bluegrass band of the same name. According to officer Robert Grandinetti, a Spokane detective obsessed with tracking the group, the FTRA is a gang of white supremist men who travel in railroad cars, particularly in the northwestern United States. He claims that homeless Vietnam veterans — who vowed to take over America's rails — founded the FTRA in a Montana bar in the 1980s. Many members sport railroad-track tattoos and wear special bandanas. They have been linked to food stamp fraud, illegal drug trafficking and theft. Some claim they mercilessly assault and murder other transients.

Members of the FTRA dispute these allegations. They claim to simply be a loosely knit club of homeless people organized for mutual support. Other homeless people not associated with the FTRA agree and claim good experiences while interacting with FTRA members. Many railroad officials say they have seen evidence that the group exists, but have not seen proof that they are a violent, criminal group. The group's lack of organization has made it difficult for authorities to track its size.

Another serial killer, Angel Resendez, eluded state police for two years and slipped through a two-month long FBI dragnet. His nine alleged murders were committed in Kentucky, Illinois and Texas. The Mexican national used weapons of opportunity found at the scenes of his crimes. His blunt-force trauma victims were often found covered with a blanket. His *modus operandi* was always the same — he struck near the rail lines, and then caught the next freight train. He became known as "The Railroad Killer."

He was disorganized and his haphazard pattern made Resendez even more elusive.

Resendez had a long criminal record, starting in 1976 at age sixteen. He served five prison terms in the United States. After every incarceration he was returned across the border to Mexico. Two years after his last recorded deportation, he killed his first known victim. In June 1999, the FBI placed "The Railroad Killer" on its "Ten Most Wanted List." Later that same month, the United States Border Patrol apprehended Resendez near El Paso, Texas. The Immigration and Naturalization Service (INS) computer system failed to identify him as a wanted man, so he was simply deported. Four more innocent people were murdered as a result of that glitch.

In July 1999, the FBI got Resendez's common-law wife to turn over ninety-three pieces of victims' jewelry that her husband had mailed to Mexico from the United States. A young Texas Ranger named Drew Carter convinced Resendez's sister to help get her brother to surrender. The serial killer turned himself in on July 13, 1999. Initially, Resendez refused to be tested by a court-appointed psychiatrist, and then chose not to accept a change of venue out of the county that produced the most executions in the United States. He finally allowed his court-appointed defense lawyers to enter an insanity plea. The jurors were not sympathetic. In May 2000, they found Angel Resendez guilty of premeditated murder. On June 27, 2006, as I was executing this chapter, "The Railroad Killer" was given a lethal injection. One of his last comments was, "I allowed the devil to rule my life."

Law enforcement officials wonder why "The Railroad Killer" surrendered so easily to a state and county that has executed more people than any other. Maybe he was insane. Resendez was a murderer and his surrender wasn't a spiritual test. But total surrender to difficult spiritual tests often produces amazing results. In the monastery, a new postulant was driving me crazy. One day, in frustration over this person's antics, I mentally screamed, "Lord, I'm going to learn to love that little jerk if it kills me." Two weeks later, he was gone. When I had cataracts and no way to pay for the necessary operation, I totally surrendered, even to the possibility of blindness. Offers of financial help poured in. Total surrender to a test often removes the test. Wave the white flag.

Yalie

Evergreener

Monk with parents, Margaret and Stan

Married Licia

"**D**ON'T YOU EVER LET ME SEE YOU DOING THAT AGAIN!" my exasperated mother yelled as the train finished crossing the road. We were out for a walk with my mother's sister, Marie, in Waseca, Minnesota, where they had grown up. The intersection we were approaching was blocked by a slow-moving freight train. I had hopped much faster trains with a full pack, so I decided to jump on the train, cross over to the other side, get off, and wait for my mom and aunt. My mom was not impressed by my maneuvers. She knew that I had been hopping freight trains for years, but actually witnessing it was too graphic for her.

Although that stunt was relatively safe, showing off can get you dismembered. Once I was in Oklahoma visiting my friend John, who was attending medical school in Tulsa. We had gone to his med student buddy's hometown of Vinita for the weekend. We fished all day and decided to go bar hopping that evening. One of the establishments we frequented was on the corner of an intersection. Behind the bar was a railroad track that went at a forty-five degree angle to the building and crossed both roads of the intersection. Not too long after we got ourselves situated and had a few drinks, I heard the warning sound of a freight train horn. I went outside and over to the road crossing closest to the oncoming train. With perfect technique, I ran alongside the fast-moving train, grabbed the ladder of a boxcar, got my legs up to speed and lifted my feet up on to the lowest rung. In mere seconds, the car I was riding crossed the other road. I reversed my procedure and gracefully exited the train.

One way to judge train speed is to watch the bolts on the wheels. If you can see them, the train is hoppable; if they are a blur, don't try it. I watched the train for a while and realized that I could not see the individual bolts. The train had to be going close to forty-miles per hour. It is not considered safe to jump a moving freight traveling over thirty-miles per hour. Had my technique not been perfect, my doctor friends would have had their first opportunity to sew limbs back on a screaming idiot. I had just enough beer in me to lower my inhibitions, but not enough to adversely affect my physical abilities. I was lucky and stupid. My friends never even saw me do it. What is the sound of one hand clapping?

Real hobos don't like show-offs. They complain about yuppie hobos who wave at people from trains and otherwise fail to keep a low profile. They think it calls too much attention to freight train riders, alerts the railroad police or *bulls* and makes it harder for genuine hobos to ride. I first read about yuppie hobos in 1987 when I was in the monastery in Los Angeles. "Have they run out of Harleys?" I thought. Now that it had become trendy, I was glad I had stopped hopping and started hoping. Men's magazines like *GQ* and *Maxim* were also promoting recreational hoboing as a manly-man survivalist sport. The *New York Times Magazine* even pushed a fall fashion "hobo chic" look. The fad slowed considerably when the two aforementioned railroad serial killers were on the loose.

I am not a full-fledged hobo, but certainly not a yuppie either, since I am neither young nor upwardly mobile. My income has usually strained to reach five figures. I am wealthy by Lao Tsu's standards, however. In the *Tao* he writes, "Those who know they have enough are rich." And I disagree with "real" hobos and don't think it hurts anyone if you show off a little at the right times. It's like anything else. You can keep the spirit of the law, while you are breaking the letter of it.

When you go through the small towns across America on a freight train, the engineer is required by law to blow the engine's horn well in advance of an intersection. The arms of the crossing signals come down with red lights flashing. Vehicles and pedestrians start to pile up to wait until the train rambles through so they can continue on with their daily rituals. One of my favorite things to do, if it was safe, was to climb on top of a freight car and pretend that I was on a float in a parade. The last time I did this was when I was entering Grand Junction, Colorado in 1997. I was riding in the third engine of a slow-moving train. I crossed over the coupling to a tanker car, climbed its ladder to a catwalk on top with a sturdy guardrail. There I sat like a parade marshal. If the local police had ever seen me doing this, they would probably have called the railroad. Citizens with cell phones might have reported me, too. Then the train could have been stopped and I could have been apprehended. But in this case, I knew that we were near the Union Pacific yard and I would be off the train before they could respond to my presence. I waved and blew kisses at the weary, restless people. When they saw me, some eyes lit up. Kindred spirits honked and waved vigorously. It made my day and possibly made theirs, too. Some perhaps long for the freedom that rail riding seems to represent. But as Jack Nicholson's character in the film *Easy Rider* observed, many Americans talk a lot about the value of freedom but are actually afraid of anyone who truly exhibits it.

Freedom isn't dumb. And life is a parade. Find your float.

Telluride's Whispering Jim had lost much of his hearing from mine blasts over the years and earned his nickname because he spoke two decibels above normal conversation level. The local legend regaled me with this tale in the Elk's Club that I managed. It sounded something like this, "THE FREIGHT TRAIN I WAS ON PULLED OUT OF GRAND JUNCTION AND HEADED WEST. WHEN IT MET UP WITH THE COLORADO RIVER AGAIN, IT CAME TO A STOP. RAILROAD *BULLS* GOT OUT AT BOTH ENDS OF THE TRAIN AND STARTED WORKING THEIR WAY TO THE MIDDLE — WITH GUNS DRAWN, SHOOTIN' TO KILL. I JUMPED IN THE RIVER AND HID IN SOME REEDS." That was during the Great Depression. Nowadays, even hobos have some civil rights, so modern railroad police are rarely as brutal as the one portrayed by Ernest Borgnine in the film *Emperor of the North*. I never hopped out East or down South, where the *bulls* are rumored to be tougher, but out West they tend to be less determined.

The important thing to remember about railroad detectives is that they are cops, more interested in coffee and donuts than kicking people off trains. With that tired generalization now in print, let's talk about the exceptions. There are still some diligent railroad detectives out there, but yardmen will almost always tell you if there is a mean *cinder dick* to contend with and will often point out a good place to hide as well.

In the Burlington Northern yards in Chicago, I got caught twice by the same detective and still managed to catch my train to Minnesota. After the *bull* kicked me out the first time, I walked along the edge of the yard just off railroad property and came upon a train ready for departure. I walked up to the locomotive and asked the engineer where they were going. He said, "Minneapolis." Just then the same detective appeared from between two freight cars. He wasn't pleased to see me again. I told him I was asking for directions to the freeway. Needless to say, he was skeptical. He took my driver's license, wrote down the data, told me how to get to the freeway, and said if he caught me again he would throw me in jail. I walked along city streets to the west end of the yard. Just past the rail yard limits was a commuter platform. It was out of sight of the train I wanted to catch, but I reasonably assumed that, since the Twin Cities-bound train was ready for departure, the next train to leave the yard was mine. It was a gamble, but I was right. I hopped on the third engine as it went by. I beamed — another hound outfoxed.

It was in this yard that I first ran into a situation that has happened to me only two or three times in my freight train riding career. The *bull* told me that a rail rider had injured himself hopping a train and sued the railroad. Such suits are nonsense because the person was trespassing. Nonetheless, when something like that happens word comes down from on high to crack down on the hobos. The railroad cops do so for a month or two, then return to their other preoccupations.

I once picked up a hitchhiker named Donn from County Clare, Ireland, who was going to Minneapolis to visit a friend. From there he was heading to Chicago. I told him that if he wanted to try freight train riding, I would help get him on one to the Windy City. He called me a week later and took me up on my offer. I picked him up and drove him to the proper yard. But when I approached our destination, I noticed two official-looking automobiles sitting by the side of the tracks. I guessed what was going on and walked up to the yard detective in one of the cars to confirm my suspicions. I asked him if some hobo had gotten hurt and sued the railroad. He said yes, took down my name, and said he'd have to throw me in jail if he saw me again. Minneapolis had always been a relatively easy place to *catch out* except this one time. I'm sure that in a few weeks it was easy again. My friend apparently didn't have the "Luck of the Irish" and had to hitch to Chicago.

The salient points to remember about railroad detectives are these: 1) don't worry too much about them. If they're hard-nosed detectives, the yardmen will either volunteer the information or will probably tell you if you ask them; 2) avoid being seen by anyone in the main tower, if at all possible; and 3) don't carry donuts — they attract a *bull* like a matador waving a cape.

Like railroad cops ignoring hobos until there is an accident, we tend to ignore God until there is a crisis in our lives. Then we moan and ask, "Where is God?" God never left. We're the ones who went "absent without leave."

There is a story about two harried parents who couldn't control their two boys. In desperation, they called in their minister to have a chat with the wildcats. The reverend decided to divide and conquer. He called the older boy into the family room, but left the younger sibling upstairs in his room. He calmly queried the young lad, "Billy, where is God?" He was sure the answer would be "heaven," but Billy gave no reply. In a louder voice, the preacher inquired, "Billy, where is God?" Silence again. Finally, the man of the cloth shouted, "BILLY, WHERE IS GOD?" Billy jumped up, clambered up the stairs, bolted into his brother's room and clamored, "Sam, Sam, we've got to get out of here. God is missing and they think we took Him."

🚂 CHAPTER 7: BOXCAR BERTHS 🚂

"The hobos built this railroad; by God, they should ride it for free."

These words allegedly came from James J. Hill, the founder of the Great Northern Railway, when he required that at least one empty boxcar be included on every train so hobos could ride. More railroads should be so enlightened. But, boxcars can be brutal. I once hopped the boxcar from hell on a Union Pacific freight train near Reno, Nevada.

I was hitchhiking to Utah and was stuck on Interstate 80, along with several other "thumbers," when the train pulled up a few hundred yards away. I hustled over to it, walked its length and selected a boxcar near the engines. If the boxcar was bad, I reasoned, I could move up to the third *unit* when the train stopped. Boxcar springs are tensioned for a load, so they normally ride somewhat rough when empty. But other things can contribute to a poor ride as well — a boxcar positioned between two other empty cars, a rough stretch of track, or an engineer who guns, then slows, the engines which causes a lot of *slack action.*

This boxcar had it all. It was so jarring that I had to stand with knees bent like a linebacker in the middle of the car away from the door, ready for motion in any direction. I could sit on my pack for only short stretches before getting shaken off. Lying on the floor, face down on my sleeping pad with my arms positioned under my body as shock absorbers was another way of briefly getting off my feet — even so, I bounced a good inch off the metal floor. It was misery incarnate. To make matters worse, this train went on seemingly forever without pulling over on a sidetrack. It ran longer without stopping than any train I've ever been on — roughly six-hours of torture. I felt like I was on a mechanical bull that wouldn't shut off. My eight-second ride became eight eternities.

Mercifully, it stopped in Elko, Nevada, some three hundred miles away, and I quickly made my exit and got into the engine. I was rewarded with a sunrise of rare beauty as we crossed the causeway on the northern portion of the Great Salt Lake approaching Ogden, Utah. But I was still beat to a pulp. Playing sixty minutes of tackle football offered less punishment than that ride. That's adventure — going through hell and living to tell about it.

Boxcars aren't just for riding, they're also used for *tagging* — illegally scrawling your moniker or other art on the side of a railcar. The *tag* I most remember was drawn in white chalk. It was a sketch of a man wearing a poncho and a sombrero taking a siesta underneath a palm tree. It was signed "Herby." I saw that *tag* all over the West and wondered if I would ever run into the hobo who did it. It turned out that he wasn't a rail rider at all. When I visited the hobo museum at Britt, Iowa in 1993, the mystery was cleared up. Herby was a railroad employee in Illinois who did his art on the job.

Boxcars are generally a good ride, but they have their dangers. The possibility of getting trapped inside if the doors shut while moving due to *slack action* or fast breaking is one of them. I read about some young men who were trapped for days inside a boxcar that contained nothing but stale beer. They lived to tell about it. Many don't. It's best to put something, like a railroad spike, in the track of the door to keep it from sliding. The doors are extremely heavy and nearly impossible for a normal human to move. Railroad employees often use a forklift to open them.

Be careful *catching out* by getting on the ladders of a boxcar. There is no place to ride — the back of the car has only a small catwalk for your feet and a rod above for a handhold. If you do it with the hope of moving to another car when the train pulls off onto a sidetrack, you could be in for a rude awakening. Remember the above boxcar I rode for six hours straight? You would be in deep trouble and would have to strap yourself to a handhold with your belt and pray without ceasing. I made this mistake on a train to Washington State on my way to school in Olympia in September of 1973.

While other parents were taking their college-aged kids to the airport, my parents brought me to the Burlington Northern freight yard in Fridley, Minnesota. My train was already pulling out as we drove into the yard. I kissed Mom goodbye, shook Dad's hand, and took off running. I had few choices if I wanted to catch that train. I grabbed the ladder of a boxcar and jumped aboard. There was absolutely no good place to ride for any length of time. I was lucky because the train went *into the hole* (pulled over on a sidetrack) fairly soon. I realized how stupid it was and never did it again, except when there was a car behind the boxcar that was a good ride but was difficult to hop on when the train was moving — like a flatcar. In this case, I would then cross over the coupling from the boxcar to the preferred car.

This maneuver is beyond dangerous and I don't recommend it. If you step on the knuckle itself, *slack action* can pinch your heel off when the cars slam together. To avoid this, you have to hold the hand grip on the boxcar, put one foot on the coupling just in front of the knuckle, let go of your handhold, step over the knuckle and on to the car to the rear — a scary leap of faith. One jarring movement by the train and you are under the wheels, blood on the tracks. But scary leaps of faith are sometimes necessary in life as well as in freight train hopping, if you want to improve your lot in life.

My friend Judy in Colorado once bragged that she had a star named after her. My rejoinder was, "That's nothing; my wife had a black hole named after me."

In railroad parlance *black hole* is the term for a tunnel. I have ridden freight trains through three of the longest in the country. On my first hop in 1973, I went through the Flathead Tunnel in Montana, west of Whitefish. At seven miles, it is the second longest tunnel in the United States. The construction of Libby Dam required rail relocation and the building of this tunnel, which opened in 1970. It was new and well lit when I went through it. When the caboose clears the entrance, a giant door closes and monstrous fans begin operation. This is supposed to blow out the diesel fumes, but they were still dreadful when I traversed. I instinctively wet my handkerchief and put it over my mouth to avoid asphyxiation.

I went through the longest tunnel in the United States in 1975. The Cascade Tunnel is 7.8 miles long and goes through the Cascade Mountains east of Everett, Washington near Stevens Pass. The Great Northern Railway built it between 1925 and 1929 to replace a shorter, higher-elevation *rat hole tunnel*. In *rat hole tunnels*, excessive fumes from the locomotives make passage dangerous. To avoid problems with smoke, tunnels need to be almost level, so the locomotives do not have to work hard while inside. Train crews carry portable respirators for use in the event of tunnel ventilation system failure or a train stalling inside the tunnel. Hobos die.

The third major burrow I have traversed is the Moffat Tunnel, fifty-miles west of Denver. At 6.2 miles, it is the sixth longest tunnel in the United States. The apex of the tunnel is 9,239 feet above sea level. It is named after Colorado railroad pioneer David Moffat who laid out the right-of-way in 1902, while seeking a better and shorter route to Salt Lake City. Moffat could not raise enough funding to build the tunnel before he died and this railroad tunnel was not opened until February 1928. Moffat Tunnel provided Denver a direct link through the Continental Divide, which shortened the distance to the Pacific coast by 176 miles.

I have an affinity for things underground, having lived in three former mining areas that later became ski areas. I ran the Elk's Club in Telluride, Colorado, which was one of the last strongholds of the area's hard-rock miners. I must have been a miner in a previous incarnation. But we are all part of God's underground. A now mythic story I once heard will help to explain what I mean.

The Germans occupied Denmark in 1941. Hitler ordered that Danish Jews be arrested and deported in October 1943. Many Danes took part in a collective effort and evacuated most of the Jews by sea to nearby neutral Sweden. The great physicist Neils Bohr was one of those rescued. He later traveled to London and the United States where he worked on the top secret Manhattan Project at Los Alamos, New Mexico. The Germans had hoped to benefit from Bohr's research. Bohr had created a substance that was needed in the process of creating hydrogen bombs. He stored the substance in a beer bottle in his refrigerator. When he fled, Bohr grabbed what he thought was the correct bottle, but it contained regular beer. The Danish Underground was sent to Bohr's former residence — now crawling with Gestapo agents — to get the intended bottle. They were not told what it contained so that if they were caught and tortured they couldn't reveal the secret. I would have balked at the seemingly senseless request and told my superiors to go buy a bottle of beer. But the Underground went in with no questions asked, got the bottle, and whisked it to safety. If the Germans had gotten hold of Bohr's discovery and figured out how to use it, they might have won the war.

We are God's underground. We are asked to do things that make no sense to us because we do not see the big picture. We don't get our ticket to the big picture until we are spiritually advanced. Until that time we have to act on faith alone.

The word "hypothermia" clanked into my mind as I sat on the flatcar of a fast moving train speeding through the plains of eastern Colorado. A sudden summer thunderstorm had soaked me to the sinews. Everything in my backpack was wet, too. It was 1974 and I was still new to freight train riding. I added two items to my list of things to always take on a rail adventure – proper raingear and plastic bags. Although it was summer, being wet in the open traveling at sixty miles per hour at night could kill you. I had two choices: a) get inside my sopping sleeping sack, or b) get off the train. At our current speed, "plan b" was not yet an option, so I slithered into my clammy cocoon and laid down. My bag was good quality and the fibers were synthetic so, in theory, they should provide warmth even when wet. That seemed to be the case except when I changed positions. But lying on a bouncing metal floor mandated frequent shifts of position and it seemed like it took forever to rewarm the wet areas around my body after I moved. While I was no longer in serious danger, I was far from comfortable.

My decision now was whether or not to get off the train earlier than I had intended. I was traveling to Lincoln, Nebraska on the Burlington Northern route. I knew the train would stop in McCook, Nebraska to change crews because I had been *set off* there in the middle of the night while sleeping on a previous hop. I could get off there, go to a laundromat, and dry my belongings. But I would probably have to wait many hours before another train came through headed for my destination. Besides, there was a young woman I was anxious to visit who was living in Lincoln, so I stayed on board. I bore a strange resemblance to a California raisin when I finally emerged from my wet wrap and disembarked nearly eight awful hours later. To make matters worse, the time with my lady friend started sweetly, but ended poorly.

The sages say if we look to external sources for happiness we will be disappointed, but when we look for happiness on the inside we will find it on the inside and on the outside.

On another rail ride, I weathered what could have been a far more dangerous storm on a Union Pacific train headed from Las Vegas to Salt Lake City. The train was totally unique to my rail-riding experience. It was nothing but engines — seven or eight of them linked together. The *rails* (railroad employees) called it a *power transfer*. The railroad was simply moving excess engines to other yards in need of them.

Riding in the engines — or the *units* as they are referred to in "railspeak" — is like moving up to first class from coach. They have heaters, bathrooms, drinking water, cushy seats, and a guaranteed smooth ride because of their weight. There are usually three engines on every main line train. The crews ride in the front *unit* and rarely come into the back ones. I rode third *units* whenever possible.

My *power transfer* raced out of Las Vegas following the I-15 freeway for a few miles until it got near the Valley of Fire State Park. Then the train veered north past Mormon Peak and up the Meadow Valley Wash. When it reached the town of Caliente, Nevada, it headed east again over a mountain pass above Beaver Dam Wash, and then dropped down into the Escalante Desert near Lund, Utah.

A wonderful thing about riding freight trains is the fact that the more beautiful the scenery, the slower the trains travel. Steep grades force them to creep through the mountains. Not in my *power transfer*. It rocketed up the pass and screamed down the other side — all that power and weight with no cars to pull. To add to this adventure, on the downhill side a fabulous flash flood occurred. Torrents of rain rushed wickedly down steep gullies, but under the elevated tracks that were well designed to deal with this fury.

It was spectacular — but only because I was safe and dry inside the *unit*. If I had been in a gully, it would have been a life and death matter. If I had been on the outside of the engine, I would have been in no serious danger, but I would have been soaked and miserable. Not having a spiritual path is like being in that gully. Having a path but not taking it to its mystic depths is like riding outside the *unit*. Will Rogers said, "Even if you are on the right track, you'll get run over if you just sit there." Meditation is sitting there without "just sitting there." It is the key that opens the door to that cozy, interior castle.

When I started meditating, it was better than drugs, sex, and rock and roll combined. When I began getting my primary inspiration internally, by tapping what Paramahansa Yogananda called the "portable paradise" within, it was like being in the cab of that engine during the flash flood. I still have mountains to climb and storms to weather, but now I ride on a *power transfer*, in my spiritual engine, on an elevated path, secured safely inside, on that cushy seat, with my feet propped up, the heaters cranked high, a cup of cool water in my hand, and I look out in awe and wonder and say:

"Good job, God."

"WARNING! Hopping freight trains is ILLEGAL AND DANGEROUS. I DO NOT RECOMMEND that you engage in this activity," states the yuppie High Tech Hobo, Glen, in large red letters on his web site. "If you are a Yuppie thrill-seeking [bleep] hole, that don't know how to act, you don't belong anywhere near railroad property," says someone on www.ftra.org, a web site dedicated to debunking media myths about the now legendary Freight Train Riders of America, "Real Freight Riders hate these yuppie [bleep] hole troublemakers more than anyone because they make things harder for everyone." An Austin, Texas computer chat room contained this response to a request from a man who was looking for locals interested in freight train hopping, "Unfortunately, the only good thing to say about train hopping is that it's a good way to get killed or crippled." In another chat room, Smitty, a Union Pacific engineer says, "You are just like any of a million other morons looking for a thrill. Our jobs are potentially dangerous enough without factoring fools and morons into the equation." The web site www.deadtrainbums.com tells of attempts by some states to pass legislation that would make it a felony to hop a freight train with imprisonment of up to one year and fines of up to four thousand dollars. And finally, my mother, Margaret, warned, "You could poke your eye out."

Freight train hopping is exceedingly dangerous. Each year about five hundred people die accidentally while trespassing on freights and rail yards around the country, according to statistics kept by the Federal Railroad Administration. Twice as many are injured. Even more trespassers are slain on freights and in *hobo jungles*, but the railroad administration doesn't keep homicide figures.

I had a near-death experience riding a freight train on the Burlington Northern line in Montana. The car carrier I was riding on was like none I had ever seen before or since. It had three levels, while the others only had two. The floor of the third level was the same height as the top of a boxcar. They hauled smaller vehicles on these tri-level rack cars so they could still clear the bridges on the lines. Today's car carriers are totally enclosed, which makes them difficult to enter. The older models had side panels (to protect the vehicles from some damage, like kids pelting them with rocks) but no roofs. The top deck of a car carrier was an especially good place to wait for a train to leave a yard. The side panels kept you out of sight and cars were tall enough so you could easily see what was happening in the yard. Once underway, in good weather, car carriers also afforded excellent views of the surrounding countryside.

It was a scintillating summer day in 1975. I was riding from Washington State to Minnesota along the Great Northern Route after graduating from

The Evergreen State College. We had just gone up the middle fork of the Flathead River and over the Continental Divide's Marias Pass near the southern tip of Glacier National Park. We were heading towards Blackfoot and the plains of eastern Montana's "Whoop-up Country," picking up speed.

I was lying in the bed of one of the Chevy Luv pickup trucks that were being transported on the upper deck of this car carrier, soaking up sunshine and scenery. Eventually, my body got stiff and I got out of the truck for a stretch. I was facing the caboose as I limbered up. A glance down at my feet showed me that I had an untied bootlace. I went down on one knee to restrap it. Just as I did so, I felt a "whoosh" over my head, saw the brief flicker of a shadow, and heard a highly amplified version of the train's ubiquitous "clickity-clack." I looked up to see that we'd just gone under a bridge. The tops of the Luv pickups on the third deck barely cleared the bottom of the bridge. I'm a lot taller than a Luv pickup. My heart raced as adrenalin rushed through my body. I slithered back into the pickup bed and tried to deny how close I had come to death. Were it not for that untied lace, I'd be known as the headless hobo.

My near-death experience is very similar to how God operates in terms of suffering. What we think of as suffering is often God tugging at our shoe laces, making us go down on our knees, forcing us to tie-up loose ends, so something even worse can be prevented.

When riding a freight train, it's extremely important to always know what's going on in front of you. Looking backwards can be hazardous to your health. It's like nostalgia. It faces you toward the caboose of life. The good old days were rarely that special. Live in the present and face forward or life might just knock your block off.

I had something in common with the Minneapolis millers (the flour millers, not the minor league baseball team), we both wanted to avoid Chicago.

In June 1975, I returned to Minnesota to work for our family construction business. In November, after our building project was completed, I hitchhiked east to visit friends before I moved to Park City, Utah. My first stop was Menomonie, Wisconsin, which is the town where I was born while my dad attended college. I looked in on my "second mother," Georgia, who still lived on the farm outside of town where my brothers and I used to spend our summers. My next stop was Toronto, Ontario in Canada to call on Barrister Bill — an old Yale buddy. The shortest route was through Chicago and Detroit, but navigating through bustling metropolitan areas can be troublesome. I decided instead to go through the Upper Peninsula (UP) of Michigan and Canada to avoid the high psychic cost of going through the Windy and Motor Cities. In the late 1800s, Minneapolis flourmill owners also decided to avoid Chicago — and the high cost of shipping flour through that city — by building a railroad through the UP.

Minneapolis grew up around Saint Anthony Falls, the highest waterfall on the Mississippi River and the end of the commercially navigable section of the river (until locks were installed in the 1960s). Following an initial burst of activity in the lumber industry, the city's economy developed around processing grain from the Great Plains. It was the leading producer of flour in the world until 1932 when interstate commerce laws changed and Buffalo, New York claimed that honor. The first railroad between Chicago and Minneapolis was completed in 1865, but mill owners felt the shipping rates were exorbitant. By the early 1870s, they were sending much of their eastbound flour to Duluth, Minnesota for transport by ship through the Great Lakes.

In September 1883, a consortium of flourmill owners in Minneapolis formed the Minneapolis, Sault Sainte Marie and Atlantic Railway in order to build a railroad between the two cities, bypassing Chicago. In Sault Sainte Marie the plan was to connect with the Canadian Pacific Railway system. The same group formed the Minneapolis and Pacific Railroad to connect Minneapolis to the Minnesota and North Dakota wheat fields. In 1887, the railroad reached Sault Sainte Marie, the Canadian Pacific spur line from Sudbury, Ontario, Canada was completed, and a new International Bridge across St. Mary's River linked them together. The first train left Minneapolis on the new railroad in January 1888. In June of that same year, the Canadian Pacific Railway acquired and consolidated several railroads to form the Minneapolis, St. Paul and Sault Sainte Marie Railway – the Soo (phonetic for Sault) Line.

For the first of three times in my freight-hopping career, I was picked up while hitchhiking by a railroad employee who helped me get on a train. This time it was on the Soo Line in Rhinelander, Wisconsin. I trundled through the Upper Peninsula to the International Bridge. It was the farthest east that I have traveled by freight train and my only freight foray into the Eastern Time Zone.

Before I walked across the International Bridge, I had to do something with a bag of the marijuana I used to smoke. I did not want to toss it, but I did not want to get busted either. I struck upon the idea to hide it in my boot wax. I heated a can of *Sno Seal* until it melted, then I put the plastic bag of contraband in the wax and let it congeal. I figured it could not be seen or smelled by dogs. The Mounties let me across the border without even inspecting my pack. As my mother would say, "You've got more luck than sense." My luck ended at the border. I had a horrible time hitchhiking in Canada. Finally, I got a ride and found out why. A convict had recently escaped from prison, hitched a ride, and killed the driver. Understandably, people were in no mood for picking up strangers.

Rail riding usually gets tougher the further east and south you go, but the route through the UP was so far out of the way that it wasn't nearly as treacherous. It's always good to have multiple travel options so you can avoid bottlenecks and deal with a variety of unanticipated circumstances. Psychologists have discovered that most humans possess multiple intelligence options as well — linguistic, logical-mathematical, musical, bodily-kinesthetic, spatial, interpersonal, intrapersonal, and naturalistic. Usually only the linguistic and logical-mathematical intelligences are tested, but it is best to develop as many as possible for maximum flexibility. Then you can, as Mr. Natural said when he saw his friend unloading a truck full of bowling balls with a pitchfork, "Use the right tool for the job."

On or off, boxcars and flatcars are two of the most difficult cars to hop when moving or *on the fly.* You can get in a boxcar door when a train is stopped the same way you get out of a swimming pool — by jumping and pushing up with your arms and swinging your legs in — but even that is hard. The floor of a boxcar is almost chest high to me and I'm over six feet tall. When the train is moving you have to throw your pack in before you hop it and, if you don't make it on, you loose your gear — but hopefully not any body parts. The best way to get into a moving boxcar is to grab the front door handle and swing, legs first, up into the car.

I only did this twice, in 1976, in the suburbs of Chicago. I had taken the subway to the Burlington Northern yard and crawled into a boxcar on a train bound for Minneapolis. It pulled out of the main Chicago yard, but went only a short distance west before it came to a stop. I got out of the boxcar to find out what was wrong. It turned out there was a *bad order* on the train — a car with a flat wheel that the engineers could feel. The steel wheels go flat when the brakes lock and the wheel grinds, metal on metal, against the tracks. After several maneuvers, they set the *bad order* off on a sidetrack. If they don't catch it in time, it could cause the train to derail.

Bad thoughts are very much like this. They can derail your train of thought if you don't set them off promptly. As the Buddha said in the Dharmapada, "As the shadow follows the body, as we think, so we become." Do whatever it takes: exercise, take a cold shower, meditate, but don't let a *bad order* thought trap you in a bad odor mood. Remember what Confucius said, "Man who break wind in church sit in own pew."

While the offending car was getting *set off,* the train blocked an intersection in a well-to-do Chicago suburb. Several well-dressed people out for walks, or bike rides, or walking home from tennis waited at the crossing with me. They had not seen me get off the train. I chatted with one of them as I watched for the train to begin moving again, so I could re-board my boxcar.

"What do you do?" he asked me.

"I'm riding this train to Minnesota."

He thought that I was joshing him and chortled. When the train started to move out, I asked everyone to step back farther from the tracks. I stood about thirty feet away from the tracks and watched the cars toward the back of the train move forward. When I spotted my boxcar, I edged closer to the tracks. The train was accelerating rapidly. As the front of my boxcar reached me, I began to sprint. I ran along the pavement next to the tracks, grabbed the front door handle, and swung up into the car. I stood quickly and waved to my slack-jawed audience. My elation soon dissolved when I didn't see my backpack. I was in the wrong car! I hopped off and ran back to the intersection.

"Wrong boxcar," I explained to the incredulous bystanders.

The speed of the train was now out of my comfort zone, but I repeated the same maneuver on the correct car. The yuppies were even more dumfounded. Since I was reasonably well dressed and hadn't had time to get filthy — as usually happens on a freight train ride — they had mistaken me for one of their own. Mistaken identity can happen to the best of us.

Once Jesus was touring heaven and stopped to chat with St. Peter at the Pearly Gates. Peter asked Jesus if he would watch the gate while he ran an errand. Jesus agreed. While he was there, a disheveled, disoriented man came to the entrance. Jesus asked if he could help him.

"I don't know. I don't remember who I am."

"Is there anything about your life that you do recall?"

"Well, I'm pretty sure that I was some sort of woodworker."

"That's a start. Is there anything else you remember?"

"Yes. I had a son in some sort of miraculous fashion."

Tears filled Jesus' eyes. He embraced the man and said, "Father!"

The old man squinted quizzically at Jesus and replied, "Pinocchio?"

A loud, belly laugh woke me from my fitful sleep on the floor of the third *unit* of a Denver & Rio Grande freight train. A railroad man was standing over me.

"And where do you think you're going?" he inquired gleefully.

"Grand Junction, I hope."

He guffawed and then left the engine.

Unsettling. Something was clearly wrong. The train was traveling too slowly and rocking too fiercely, sure signs that we weren't on the main line. A reading of the stars told me we were heading south, not east to Grand Junction, Colorado. I was on a work train on some secondary line. Where I was I did not know, but I had a mysterious craving for lime Jell-O with mini-marshmallows.

I saw the lights of a small town in the distance. I decided that my best course of action was to get off the train, hike over to the town, and find out where on this planet I was. Getting off the train was no problem as it ambled along at low speed. It was still the middle of the night when I reached the sleepy town. A gas station — closed for the night — had a large map of the region posted on an outside wall. Oh my heck! I was on US Highway 89 in Ephraim, Utah — right in the middle of the dreaded "Mormon Triangle."

The Mormon Triangle is an area bounded by Interstates 15 and 70 and US Highway 6. I knew it well. I often traveled through the Mormon Triangle as I commuted back and forth between Brian Head and Park City, Utah. For a few months, I simultaneously served as a Planning Commissioner in Park City, Utah and as Town Manager/Planner/Chief Budget Official/Fireman/ Deputy Marshal/Back-up Garbage Collector of Brian Head, Utah. The two towns were five hours apart. The Planning Commission met on Thursday night; so I would drive up on Thursday, do work for Brian Head in Salt Lake City on Friday and party in Park City over the weekend. I was still a card-carrying member of the Immoral Minority.

People have been known to disappear in the Mormon Triangle only to reappear years later with eight wives and thirty-nine children in polygamist-friendly Colorado City, Arizona. To the north of Ephraim was Moroni — named after the patron angel of the Church of Jesus Christ of the Latter Day Saints. (My computer's spell check suggested some surprisingly judgmental alternatives for Moroni.) To the south was Manti — home of one of the ubiquitous Mormon Temples.

I decided that my best bet was to hitchhike south to Salina and catch Interstate 70 east to Grand Junction. Rides were scarce and my beard announced that I probably wasn't a Mormon. Apparently, for most drivers, a potential convert wasn't worth the risk of death at the hands of some mad hitchhiker. I made it to Manti. Then came Sterling. Gunnison. Centerfield.

Axtell. Finally, I got to Salina and out of the Triangle. I phoned Telluride, Colorado to have a back-up bartender cover for me at the Elk's Club and thumbed my way home — a day late and a tad wiser for the experience.

I hopped another wrong train out of Seattle that I thought was going on the old Great Northern Hi-Line route across the northern states. I had just graduated from college in 1975, but to do so I had to stay a quarter longer than I knew I could handle emotionally. After the commencement ceremonies — in a brain funk — I went with my parents and my uncle and aunt on a disastrous trip to Victoria Island in Canada. After visiting other friends in British Columbia, I was now trying to *catch out* to the Midwest. My previous hop on the Hi-Line in 1973 had begun in western Washington and I didn't know the rails in the Puget Sound area very well. The only yardman in Seattle that I queried did not tell me that I had to change trains in Everett, Washington for passage over the Cascade Mountain Range. It should have been easy to figure out.

In Everett, at least a dozen other riders disembarked from my freight and walked toward the north end of the yard. One small gruff man was carrying an axe. I did not feel like going his way. I was alone in a comfortable boxcar distilling pure denial. In reality, I was rolling nowhere. I finally realized — too late — that I had to do what the other hobos had done, transfer to an eastbound train to Spokane. I had a full day to explore the seedy sections of Everett before the next train headed out.

There are false spiritual teachers out there who can also give you bad information. It can be unintentional. Unfortunately, the teachings of the avatars that founded the great religions often devolve because people of lesser spiritual stature and larger ego think they can toy with them. You can't blame Christ for Christianity — or Moses or Krishna or Buddha or Mohammed for the current state of their respective religions. Discrimination is imperative in order to find a teaching in its purest form. Get multiple opinions about spiritual paths as well as freight train destinations.

A state trooper pulled over slowly as I was hitchhiking in Minersville, Utah in 1977. He's going to run a computer check on me, I thought to myself, to see if there are any warrants out for my arrest. This had happened to me many times before, so I got out my driver's license, opened up the passenger side door, and handed it to him.

"No, I don't need to see that. Hop in. I'll give you a ride."

I'd been hitching for over ten years and had never had a ride offer from a cop. How could I decline?

"Where are you heading?" he asked.

"Milford. I'm going to a State Transportation meeting."

"Me too! I'm the head of the Highway Patrol for this region."

I told him that I worked for Brian Head, Utah. A hitchhiking Town Manager was out of his realm of experience, so the officer was incredulous at first, but our destinations were indeed the same. The steepest paved road in Utah accessed our ski resort town situated at ten thousand feet. Some of the switchbacks desperately needed new guardrails — only the rebar inside crumbling cement posts held them up. I was going to encourage our regional Transportation Czar to make our situation a high priority.

Milford is one of my favorite Utah towns. In the early 1870s, cattle ranching began in the area. With only a few shacks built in the hills near mines, residents in the 1880s described Milford as a "perfect mud hole," or the "perfection of desolation." During the 1880s, Milford became the railroad terminus for the Southern Utah Railroad, which made it an important supply station and the shipping center for local mines and ranches. After two failed attempts, the line was extended to Caliente, Nevada in 1901, linking Utah to California. Milford, a *division point* on the railroad, was incorporated in 1903. The Union Pacific Railroad, which absorbed the smaller rail lines, is still the community's largest employer.

The trooper and I got to Milford an hour early and decided to get a bite at the Hong Kong Cafe. This establishment had been in an Asian family's hands since unskilled Chinese laborers — derogatively called coolies — built the railroad. The food was exceptional. We had a great meal and a nice chat. After the meeting (where our Transportation Czar comfortingly told me that the guard rails only had psychological value anyway) the officer offered me a ride home. I had to decline.

The reason I was hitching to this meeting was because I had another meeting with the State Health Department early the next day in Salt Lake City. There was no way that I could attend the meeting in Milford, stay awake for a five-hour drive to Salt Lake, and be coherent for my morning rendezvous. I knew Milford was a railroad town where the Union Pacific stopped to change crews. I had decided that my best course of action was to hitch to Milford for meeting number one and then catch a freight train to Salt Lake City that evening. I could sleep on the train, clean up at the Greyhound bus terminal in Salt Lake City the next morning, put my pack in a locker and take a city bus to meeting number two.

"Thanks," I told the trooper, "But I'm going to stay here and catch a freight train to Salt Lake City. I have an important meeting at the State Capitol in the morning."

He bade me an incredulous goodbye. Many in conservative southern Utah thought the people in our ski resort town were heathens from hell. I'm sure a tale about a hitchhiking, freight-riding town manager did little to change their minds.

"You can't make both meetings," my intellect had initially insisted.

"Recant your can't," was my intuition's reply; "think outside the little boxes you create to file your life away."

Hafiz writes,

> I rarely let the word "No" escape
> From my mouth
> Because it is so plain to my soul
> That God has shouted, "Yes! Yes! Yes!"
> To every luminous movement in existence.

Like I shouted "Yes, yes, yes" to the luminous movement of the approaching locomotive headlamps later that evening.

*C*inder Dick. The colorful, hobo expression for a railroad detective came to mind when a man with a holstered gun entered the third engine of the freight train I was trying to hop in Salt Lake City, Utah. The man's first words confirmed my suspicion.

"How'd you like to spend the night in jail?"

"OK," I answered as I stood up. A good, low syllable answer is always smart under such circumstances. As Will Rogers said, "Never miss a good chance to shut up."

Hopping freight trains is illegal — it's trespassing. Going to jail is a potential consequence. I accepted that, although I've only been in jail once in 1971 in the St. Croix River town of Hudson for the heinous crime of hitchhiking on a Wisconsin freeway. I had just spent a weekend assisting my "second mother" in Menomonie, Wisconsin. No good deed goes unpunished. I didn't have the cash on me to pay my fine and would have served my time, but I was about to go to Europe and had much to do. I called my dad who, thankfully, drove twenty-six miles from Minneapolis to bail me out.

When I was busted in Salt Lake City, I was sitting on the stairs leading down to the engine's bathroom, so the *bull* didn't know how big I was. When my six-foot, four-inch, two hundred-pound frame got fully vertical, he mellowed considerably. He still made me get off the train and sit in his passenger car at the north end of the yard until the train departed.

I kicked myself for being so lazy and boarding the train too early. The Denver and Rio Grande yard in Salt Lake City was familiar terrain. I was a "frequent flyer" to Grand Junction, Colorado along this rail route over the Wasatch Mountains. I knew where to hide until the train pulled out — in a shed on the south end of the yard. A yardman had once shown me this warming hut on a nippy, winter night. It had three normal sides holding up the roof, but there was no fourth side. Inside the building was a giant heater — as tall I am. The yardman showed me the button that turned it on for five-minute intervals. It was so hot, that I had to rotisserate to keep from scorching. I used that shed many times after that, even in the summer — not for warmth, but because it kept me out of sight of the yard tower. *Cinder Dicks* are supposed to watch for hobos from those towers. Some actually do.

On this particular escapade, my friend Steve dropped me off by at the north end of the yard under the 21st South Bridge, leaving me a long hike on a scalding day to my shelter. As I hoofed toward my hideout, I passed the train to Denver — engines on, ready to go. In plain sight and broad daylight, I climbed into the third engine, a foolish whim. The detective later told me that the engineer saw me and called him immediately.

When I finished second-guessing myself, I turned my monkey mind on the *bull*. Why didn't he just kick me out of the yard instead of making me wait in his car? He was smart, I guess. I would have snuck back in and caught the train from another spot in the complex. He knew the tricks. I finally gave up any hope of getting on that freight.

"Where are you trying to get to?" he asked.

"Telluride, Colorado. I manage the Elk's Club there." (Let them know you work.)

"My father was an Elk."

"Really? I took the job so I could meet the old-timers in town. It's one of their last strongholds." (Let them know what a regular guy you are.)

My train finally rambled out of sight. Then, to my complete surprise, the *bull* drove me down a dirt road to a boxcar on another train.

"Hop in there," he said. "This is a priority train. We call them *hot shots*. It's going to pass the train you were trying to catch. Just stay out of the engines."

Cinder Dicks! They're not as bad as the movies make them out to be.

I think about this adventure whenever I find myself struggling with a major change in my life. It helps me to stop my mental gyrations and surrender, knowing that God is just taking me off one train and putting me on a *hot shot* that will fast forward my spiritual evolution.

God! She's not as bad as religions make her out to be.

"I just stole this car. Hop in. I'm heading for to Salt Lake City."

I hopped in. It was not the first time I'd ever ridden in a stolen car, but it was the first time anyone announced the fact with the first sentence out of his mouth.

"I was on a work release program at a golf course in Delta and saw this baby with a full tank of gas and the keys in it. I decided to take an early parole."

Delta is a town in western Colorado. "This baby" was a just-out-of-the-box Cadillac. I knew it was stolen just by looking at him. I didn't care. He immediately showed me his driver's license, which had "FOR PRISON VEHICLES ONLY" printed across the front. He seemed to need to verify his story. I didn't ask for a second piece of identification.

"When I get to Salt Lake City, I'm going to sell this Caddy, buy a Harley, and mix in with biker trash."

Another fairy tale awaiting an unhappy ending.

"The name's Rex. How far are ya goin'?"

"Southern Utah. I'll ride with you as far as Green River."

"No problem. I could use the company."

That was certainly true, because he kept speeding and I had to keep reminding him to slow down. The speed didn't bother me, but as I pointed out to Rex, getting pulled over by a State Trooper and showing him a prison ID would not advance his game plan. Luckily, we got to Green River unapprehended. I bought him the first beer he'd had in five years and gave him a little money for gas. Aiding and abetting? I suppose so, but a brand new Cadillac in a golf course parking lot with the keys in it is an attractive nuisance. The owner should have been issued a ticket.

The "on-the-lam-man" had picked me up in Fruita, a small town outside Grand Junction, Colorado. For some reason, I've been stuck there while hitchhiking multiple times. Another highly unusual experience also originated in Fruita. I was "thumbing" in the shade of the Fruita Bridge — with very little success — for almost an hour when the horn of a freight train engine came out of nowhere. It was just sitting there, hidden from sight by a massive berm that rose between the tracks and the freeway.

I was startled at first, and then I started salivating like one of Pavlov's dogs when I realized that this could be my ticket out of there. I scaled the berm and checked the tracks. It was a coal train heading west. I knew it had to go toward Salt Lake City, my destination at the time. I walked up and talked to the engineer who said they were going to a coal washing plant near Helper, Utah to leave their load and then take the engines into Helper. (They spray granite dust in the coalmines to keep flammable coal dust down. The granite dust then needs to be removed from the coal.) Getting to Helper, a railroad town where they add extra engines called *helpers* before crossing Soldier Summit, would be immensely helpful. Coal hoppers are a horrible mess to ride in and the engines were going further than the cars, so I climbed into the third *unit.* I spent the night in a yardmen's warming shack in the Helper yard and caught the next freight train to the Great Salt Lake in the morning.

The berm in Fruita kept me from seeing that coal train while I sat hitching almost right next to it. It was like cognitive blindness. The famous Chilean biologist, Humberto Maturana, claims perception is structurally determined — we perceive only what our brain and nervous system allow us to perceive. We are like a machine in this regard. Our structure was developed in our past, so at any given moment, we perceive only and exactly what our past allows. Aboriginals, who were shown photographs taken of them, were not able to pick out their own images because their brains were not wired for that technology. Fortunately, we are machines that can learn. Change the machine.

There are basically two types of people — those who divide people into two types and those who don't. Hobos make a big distinction between themselves and bums. A hobo mentioned in Maury Graham's book *Tales of the Iron Road* illustrates the difference with the following story. A bum would come to the back door of a farmhouse and say, "Lady, can you spare a bite to eat?" A hobo, on the other hand, would say, "Lady, could I chop that wood over there in exchange for something to eat?" True hobos, Graham says, hate being called bums, who they consider to be shiftless, lazy and generally worthless. Bums also move about more nomadically as opposed to hobos who tend to follow fairly well defined circuits. Hobos never force themselves on anyone, Graham claims, and always consider others. They have a natural courtesy and kindness, he believes. I have experienced that courtesy.

I once hopped on the third *unit* of a freight train in Lincoln, Nebraska that I thought was heading west. Apparently, they forgot to diesel-up the engines, so they took them off the line of cars they were attached to and over to the fueling bay. This was an intensely lighted area and I suspected that I would have railroad employees coming to visit. I hid in the engine's bathroom with the door slightly ajar, so I could see if anyone entered the cab of the engine. Another hobo did. He sat on the stairs going down to the bathroom while I hid a few feet away. He was unaware of my presence, but I didn't want to stay in the cramped bathroom — with all my gear — forever. When the train started moving, I opened the door. The man leapt to his feet. He thought I was a railroad detective.

"I ain't gonna touch nothing."

"It's OK. I'm riding this beast, too."

He was much relieved, said his name was Neanderthal, and offered me a drink from his pint of whiskey. We chatted for a few minutes, and then he announced that he would move up to the second *unit* and ride there, leaving me undisturbed. Since I had gotten into the third *unit* first, he respected my claim — hobo courtesy.

My wife and I experienced hobo courtesy in November 2009 when we paid a visit to the former King and Queen of the Hobos, Tuck and Minneapolis Jewel, in Minnesota. Jewel regaled us with stories of her early days at the Britt Hobo Convention (described in Chapter 23). She thoughtfully sent us a steam train postcard within a week. Tuck gave me a railroad tie *date nail* with my birth year on it. After finding out that my four-foot, nine-inch tall wife had never ridden a freight train, he suggested that I put her in a five-gallon bucket and lift her into a boxcar.

Hobos are Taoists but may not know it. Both view success in similar ways. In Chapter 20 of Stephen Mitchell's translation of the *Tao Te Ching*, the legendary Lao Tsu writes,

> Stop thinking, and end your problems.
> What difference between yes and no?
> What difference between success and failure?
> Must you value what others value,
> Avoid what others avoid?
> How ridiculous!

Hobos have checked out of the materialistic mainstream for many of the same reasons as a man I met back East. I was taking a class called "Abnormal Psychology" at Yale and we took a field trip to a Connecticut Valley mental institution. When we walked in the door, dressed in our sport coats and ties, a patient looked at us, shook his head and said, "Hey man, we read the newspapers. We think you're the ones that are nuts."

Some people divide seekers into two types, religious and spiritual. The religious are deemed more fundamentalist and the spiritual somehow more advanced. I am the type of person who subdivides the second category into two types, spiritual and mystic. Sometimes spiritual people get trapped into seeking spiritual entertainment instead of spiritual attainment or spiritual information, which doesn't foster the spiritual formation of the mystic.

People interested in spiritual entertainment and information read all the right books, go to all the right lectures, and attend services at upbeat churches that feature positive thinking. There is nothing wrong with this. It's a step in the right direction, but, as with any step or change, there is always a danger of getting stuck. They could become spiritual bums in the sense that they always want a spiritual handout. They might not want to work for their advancement, expecting their inspiration to always come from outside themselves.

Mystics seeking spiritual attainment and formation are willing to work for their enlightenment. They meditate and get fed from that reservoir inside themselves. They are spiritual hobos. And if you want to be a spiritual hobo, you have to spend a lot of time on your bum.

There is a Taoist story about a farmer whose prize stallion got loose. His neighbor said, "That's bad." The farmer said, "Maybe it is; maybe it isn't." Two days later the horse returned with a herd of wild horses in his wake. The neighbor said, "That's good." The farmer said, "Maybe it is; maybe it isn't." While trying to break one of the horses, the farmer's son shattered his leg. The neighbor said, "That's bad." The farmer said, "Maybe it is; maybe it isn't." A week later the army came through the area conscripting every able-bodied young man. The farmer's son was not fit for service.

A similar series of events propelled me out of Telluride, Colorado. I lost a town council election in April 1981 by one vote under bizarre circumstances. That loss pried me out of an incredible town I thought I would never leave. Before I left, however, I caught one more train to Utah.

My best friend from first grade, Bill, was getting married in Park City, Utah in June 1981. Jo, a mutual friend of ours, also wanted to attend the festivity. Jo and I were the hottest country swing dancers in the Eastern San Miguel County Mosquito Control District. I once applied my warped sense of humor on her father's affliction. When Jo's parents visited from Australia, her father got a terrible case of bronchitis and coughed horribly. When he did so, Jo and I would break out into my variation of the Australian anthem "Waltzing Matilda" called "Walking Pneumonia." Jo's father pretended to be angry but, being of the same ilk, clearly enjoyed the wit.

Jo was up for a hoboing adventure. We hitchhiked to Grand Junction, Colorado and *caught out* on a Denver and Rio Grande freight train to Salt Lake City. Our train that day was a string of *piggybacks* or highway truck trailers on specially built flatcars. These are *hotshots*, but not ideal to ride, as they offer painfully little protection from the elements. If the weather went bad, we'd be the ones with walking pneumonia. Even if the weather were cooperative, it would be difficult to get out of the wind except by getting behind the wheels of a trailer. Speed was more important than comfort to us at that point, so we decided to *hotshot* to Zion.

Jo had acquired the nickname "Pigpen" when she lived in Park City. She walked about without shoes and was often covered with dust up to her knickers. She was equated with the Charles Schultz character and given the unflattering moniker. Before long on this trip, she was every bit the character and tired of the wind whipping that we were receiving on our *piggyback* ride. I suggested that we get off when they changed crews and added extra engines in Helper, Utah. Jo adamantly agreed.

Helper is one of my favorite places. It was once known as the "Gentile Town in Zion." Butch Cassidy's Wild Bunch roamed at will. A polygamist named Teancum Pratt homesteaded the area in 1881. The Denver and Rio

Grande Railroad (D&RG) bought the right-of-way from Pratt in 1883 when they discovered coal beds in the area. The D&RG soon built a depot, a hotel, a fifteen-stall roundhouse, a large water tank, a steam plant, and a non-denominational chapel (for all to use except union activist Mother Jones). Following a strike in 1903-04, many coal miners who had been evicted from mining camps came to Helper where they started businesses and became community leaders. Helper has always had a diverse ethnic population, served as the hub for the mining camps and, occasionally, as strike headquarters. Helper incorporated in 1907 and voted to go "wet" and serve liquor in 1911. Jack Dempsey boxed there. Houses of ill repute abounded until the 1970s. The Helper Hotel (built in 1914; purchased by the railroad in 1942; sold to the city in the 1980s) now is home to the excellent Western Mining and Railroad Museum.

Jo and I decided to get some food before we hitchhiked the rest of the way to Park City. We found a grandmotherly place decorated with frilly curtains and stuffed bears on Ivy Street called The Pie Shop. We were filthy and horribly out of place, but too hungry to care. Jo ordered and went straight to the rest room. When she returned she looked presentable. I took my turn in the bathroom: it was a mess. The coating of diesel dirt that once covered Jo's face and hair now coated the sink. I tried to clean it — as I'm sure Jo did — but it needed serious cleansers. It looked even worse after I finished washing up. We ate and left the unsuspecting Mormon lady who owned the place an extra large tip to assuage our guilt. I am sure that she thought we lived in pigpens.

I cringe when people call themselves sinners. Sin is simply looking in the wrong direction for happiness. It is something that we do, but it is not who we are. It's like our railroad grime. It comes off with a good karmic scrubbing. And God will scour the sink for us.

It was midday when I approached a Union Pacific yardman in East Los Angeles to ask if the freight train he was building was going to Las Vegas, Nevada.

"Yes, it is," he said, but warned, "This is a *hot yard*. The yard detective has seen you, and he's on his way to arrest you. You'd better *low line*."

Yardmen rarely help railroad cops. It's a labor-management thing. Yardmen are labor. Yard detectives are management. I started to leave in the direction I had come in from in order to lure the *bull* to the wrong side of the yard. As soon as I was screened from the tower by a line of freight cars, I reversed direction. The old game of cat and mouse — or *bull* and matador — was on.

I headed for a four-foot tall chain-link fence that separated the railroad property from a freeway. Several lines of freight cars sat idly on tracks between the fence and me. They would provide good cover, but that also meant climbing up car ladders, across catwalks and down ladders on the other side for each line of cars. Even though I was in a hurry, I had to be very careful. I knew better than to try to go under a freight car. They can be jerked unexpectedly and chop off limbs. I preferred to spend time in a jail rather than time in a hospital. When I crossed the last string of cars, I still had three empty tracks and a dirt road to cross before getting to the fence.

I checked the tracks for freight cars that can roll quietly and dangerously through a freight yard. While doing so, I saw a pickup truck about a hundred yards away roaring up the dirt road. I sprinted for the fence and scaled it as the cop screeched to a stop. I continued down a shrub-covered embankment as the *bull* disembarked. He said nothing, but gave me a menacing "I'll-get-you-next-time look" through the enveloping dust cloud that he had created. It was not a win-win situation.

I went down to the edge of the freeway, through a tunnel under the railroad yard, up the next entrance ramp, and over to a Denny's restaurant that was next to the yard. From a window in there, I could watch developments in the yard. When the Vegas-bound engines went by to hook-up to the front of the rail cars, I would make my move to *catch out*. I had to wait a long time.

I had just quit my job as manager of the Telluride Elk's Club, flown to California, and was leaving Los Angeles after attending my first Self-Realization Fellowship Convocation in August 1981. I had been practicing their meditation methods for several months. They worked as advertised and I added them to the bag of tricks that I thought was making me happy. I soon realized that meditation was about the only thing that I was doing that didn't have negative side effects. Then I realized that the less I practiced my other bad habits the better I meditated. It was hard to quit those other things in a hedonistic ski resort town. Buckminster Fuller said, "Environment is stronger than will." This is especially true when you are new to a spiritual path. I made a decision to move back to Minnesota. But first I wanted to attend this Convocation. It was transformative.

Finally, three engines went by. When I saw the cars on the first track rock violently backwards, I knew the *units* were attached. The train hissed and lurched and started picking up speed. I shouldered my backpack and hustled out the door. I went behind the Denny's and along the side of the neighboring warehouse, where I was out of sight of the tower. I got to the edge of the warehouse next to the tracks and peered around the corner. No *bull* in sight.

As I've said before, catching a train *on the fly* is tricky. I started walking between the warehouse and the tracks, moving in the opposite direction from the train. I began *rolling the train*, looking for a decent car to ride before the train got going too fast. They were all grain cars. They slope in at both ends and if they have a metal platform, they're a good ride. If they don't have a platform, there are only steel beams to straddle. You literally have to tie yourself down; otherwise you might fall asleep and slide off onto the wheels. It could ruin your incarnation.

The train was getting up to the maximum speed that I felt comfortable hopping with a backpack. I reversed direction and ran until I was almost up to speed with the train. I chose a ladder at the back of a grain car and fixed my attention on a head-high rung. As it went by me, I grabbed it tightly — still running so my momentum wouldn't throw me into the coupling and under the wheels. I ran a few more steps until I was balanced enough to jump up onto the bottom rung. A strap on my backpack broke and pitched me forward precariously — thankfully, the grain car had a platform.

Grain cars often have a hole in the back that leads to an empty, cave-like space. Even though I am over six-feet tall, I knew from my years of rail riding experience that I could squeeze inside. I put one leg into the hole and followed with my head and upper torso. I drew in my remaining leg and pulled my backpack in on top of me. I was virtually invisible.

Two years later, I squeezed my oversized ego into a monastic cave and became invisible to the world. My dad thought that I was escaping life but, with few distractions and nowhere to run, it was like a demon-facing, moral intensive care unit. My rationalizations crumbled under the onslaught of the jackhammer of introspection. I became convinced that I was something I had long denied. I was a womanizer. I had virtually no contact with women for seven years and I did not date for a full year after getting out of the monastery. I didn't want to fall back into that ugly pattern again.

🚂 CHAPTER 20: GANDY DANCER 🚂

The Merriam-Webster dictionary says that a *gandy dancer* is a laborer in a railroad-track-maintaining *section gang*. True enough. But the dictionary also states that the origin of the term is unknown. Not true. Many of the tools that *section gangs* used were made by the Gandy Tool Company of Chicago — hence the true origin of the nickname. While I never worked on a *section crew*, I was a *gandy dancer* by proxy — a *section foreman* actually, the one who oversees track construction and repair.

I was on a trip from Tacoma, Washington to Salt Lake City, Utah. My uncle Dayle had arranged a ride for me to Portland, Oregon. I was hitchhiking from Portland to Hermiston, Oregon to catch a freight train when it stopped to change crews before crossing the Blue Mountains. This is a good practice because small yards have no yard detective. And, if there is a long wait, there usually is a local color cafe or tavern nearby — rarely the case in a big city yard. It is altogether a more pleasant experience. Ask any yardman where to find these crew-change *division points.*

Oddly enough, my first ride out of Portland was from a man who worked for the Union Pacific — the very railroad I was planning to ride for free. When Gary found out my scheme, he said he'd see what he could do. He was going to The Dalles, which is about an hour out of Portland. Trains usually race through The Dalles at speeds far too fast to hop. Without telling me his plan, Gary drove down to the yardmaster's office, took me inside, and announced to the yardmaster:

"This guy is a *section foreman.* He's going to *section foreman* school in Salt Lake City. Would you stop the next train for him?"

"Sure, no problem," the yardmaster replied.

I was flabbergasted. I was the alleged *section foreman.* Despite my shock, I kept a cool cover. I picked up a union magazine and flipped through it trying to find topics of conversation that I might need to use later. (I learned that unionized fish strike more.) Gary continued talking with the yardmaster.

We had a good hour before the next train came through, so Gary took me to his trailer. I showered and we went out for a few beers. When the train was about to arrive, the yardmaster radioed Gary at the tavern and we headed down to the tracks. The train stopped, I thanked Gary, and got in the third *unit.* The conductor came back to make sure I was comfortable and the train rumbled away. I rode to the Idaho border and then got off at dawn to hitchhike.

I used this scam one other time in my career in November 1983 on my farewell tour before I become a monk. After visiting my Yale buddy, Matt, and his family in the Black Hills in South Dakota, I had hitchhiked into Cheyenne, Wyoming. It was nighttime and a blizzard had closed Interstate 80 west of Laramie due to drifting snow, as often happens. I didn't want to be held up, so I simply looked up the Union Pacific phone number in the Yellow Pages and gave them a jingle.

"This is Wayne Iverson," I said calmly, "I'm headed to *section foreman* school in Salt Lake City and the roads are closed. Can I catch the next train?"

"You bet," was the reply. "The next train leaves in half an hour."

I beat the crew to the yard and found my train. A yardman invited me into the yard office to keep warm, but I didn't think I could fake being a *section foreman* for very long. I made a comment about a piece of railroad equipment called a *cherry picker* in order to sound legitimate before hunkering down in the third *unit*.

Lying is almost always wrong, but in rare cases it may even be desirable. I have lied to my Alzheimer's clients in order to ease their muddled minds. Truth does no harm. For example, imagine you were sitting in a park when an obviously battered woman ran up to you and panted: "My husband is after me. He says he is going to kill me and I believe him this time. I am going to hide in these bushes. Please don't tell him where I am."

When the husband came would you — knowing it was wrong to lie — point to where the woman was located? You would be forced to discern between fact and truth. Not saying anything might get you killed. Telling him where the woman was might get her killed. The facts in both scenarios would cause harm. A correct response would be to point in the opposite direction and say: "She ran down that path."

Otherwise, when you died, and wondered aloud why you ended up in Hades, you might be told: "Your refusal to lie cost a woman her life. A life is more important than a commandment!"

Photo by Tom Lee

Photo by Tom Lee

CHAPTER 21: THE HUMP

W hen I first saw a sign that read "Do Not Hump" on a boxcar, I knew I had to have one. I didn't know what it meant at the time, though I thought it sounded like the title of a Religious Right abstinence lesson. I found out later that in railspeak *hump* has three basic meanings. A little yardbird told me about the first kind of *hump*.

"That there engine is a yard switcher. We use her to build trains for departure and break up the incoming trains, if they need it. When we build a train, the switcher picks up a few cars, and then backs them down the track we're building the train on. It speeds up, and then brakes. The car next to the engine isn't coupled so when the switcher stops, it, and the other cars with it, keeps on a-goin'. The rolling cars are called *midnight creeps* and are dangerous because you can't usually hear them coming down the tracks. If you're not looking, they can kill you. They roll until they ram the other cars on the track and the couplings lock. That's what we call *humping*. If the car has fragile cargo, we don't want to bash her like that, so we put those "Do Not Hump" signs on her."

Many modern yards have a large, built-up mound with a single track on one side called *the hump*. The switcher engine pushes the cars over this man-made hill and the brakeman uncouples them. The cars roll down *the hump* and are switched electronically from the tower to one of a myriad of tracks that branch out at the bottom. That's the second meaning of *hump*.

Thirdly, the Continental Divide is also referred to as *the hump*. Going over it in winter is a rite of passage — like crossing the equator on an ocean-going vessel. I crossed over *the hump* in Wyoming on the winter ride where I masqueraded as a *section foreman*. The pass is low in elevation in that state and you actually cross it twice. There's an area called the Great Divide Basin between Rawlins and Rock Springs. The water flows in there and can't make up its mind whether to go to the Atlantic or Pacific Ocean. It just stays in the Red Desert and evaporates like our chances in life if we are unwilling to cross any humps. The Continental Divide circles around it and you get a double *hump* on that route.

After we went over the two *humps*, we crossed the border into Utah and I could see Interstate 80 about a half-mile from the tracks. I knew if I got off of the train there, walked to the freeway, and hitchhiked, I could be at my destination in Park City in an hour or two. If I stayed on the train until it stopped in Ogden, I would have to hitch through Salt Lake City and double back east again to get to Park City — an all-day endeavor. I decided I would jump off the train right away.

I was riding in an engine, which has steep steps and side rails instead of ladders. It was winter and the lower steps were iced up. The snow along the tracks was deep. The speedometer in the engine indicated that the train was going twenty miles per hour — slow enough to get off safely in normal conditions, but these were not normal conditions. I carefully inched my way down the stairs until I was on the slick bottom rung. Then, while still holding tightly to the side rails, I dropped my feet to the ground and started running. You must do this to get up to speed with the train before you let go of your handhold. Otherwise, you might stumble and get pulled under the train.

Concentrating as I was on my footing on the slippery steps, I forgot another very important rule: scope out the tracks ahead of the train for obstacles before jumping off. We were rapidly approaching a narrow bridge with insufficient room between the cars and the trussing. I had to either jump back on those frozen steps or let go of my handhold before I had my balance. I quickly chose the latter. I took two or three out-of-control, bounding leaps and finished with a face plant in the deep snow. I surfaced with a dusting of white and a belly laugh. My only damage was a deep cut in my knee where it hit some sharp cinders under the snow. I could have used stitches, but there wasn't a doctor nearby. The cut left a distinct mark when it healed — my red badge of courage. Or stupidity.

The sign I finally procured said, "Switch Carefully, Do Not Hump." As I stared at it on my bedroom ceiling, I often thought that those were good words to live by. Don't go bashing and crashing your way through existence. Life is a dance, not a race.

M y 1983 farewell tour of the western part of the country was prompted by my acceptance into Self-Realization Fellowship's monastic order. I did not expect to see any of my friends again and I wanted to say goodbye. I rode three freight trains on that bittersweet journey. The first was when I was headed to Oklahoma to say adios to my Yale pal John, who was now married and a doctor in Bartlesville. I was hitchhiking west out of Pueblo, Colorado when an employee of the Santa Fe Railroad picked me up. He informed me that the trains changed crews in La Junta, Colorado. That meant an easy hop out of a small town. The yard was immediately adjacent to the main highway. A yardman (yardwoman actually) told me when the next train to Newton, Kansas was leaving. I had a few hours to kill, so I went to a cozy restaurant to wait.

La Junta means junction or meeting place. It was originally a spot where several Indian trails intersected. In 1832, Charles Bent, his brother, William, and Ceran St. Vrain built a fort near a ford across the Arkansas River that became known as the "Castle on the Plains." They were the first white settlers in the area and Bent's Old Fort was the principle trading post on the Mountain Route of the Santa Fe Trail until 1849. Kit Carson supplied the fort with buffalo meat. Its strategic location on the then Mexican border made it the ideal staging area for General Stephen Watts Kearney's invasion of that country in 1846, when our Manifest Destiny policy encouraged us to steal land from our neighbors.

In the 1870s, the Santa Fe Railroad won a long, bitter battle with the Kansas Pacific Railroad for supremacy in southeast Colorado. La Junta boomed when railroad construction halted there temporarily in December 1875. Calamity Jane plied her trade in town. In 1878, La Junta was made a railroad *division point* and the first shops were built the following year. La Junta was actually located at the junction of three *division points* of the Santa Fe — once again living up to its name. It had a Harvey House restaurant and a hospital built to serve railroaders. Development in La Junta for the next hundred years was primarily dependent on the railroad.

In October 1903, two men tore up some nearby tracks before a train approached and robbed it. A five thousand dollar reward was offered for their capture. Years later, one of them was bragging in Portland, Oregon about the crime. He was reported to the police, sent back, and convicted. It pays to keep your mouth shut.

The railroad man who picked me up hitchhiking in 1983 said specifically that I should not ride in the engines and that I should get off before Newton, Kansas because they usually did thorough sweeps of the trains there looking for felons. Naturally, I rode into Newton on an engine. I had no close encounters. I hitchhiked through southeastern Kansas to Bartlesville. The valleys I traversed were incredible: the trees were in their prime fall colors, while winter wheat poked its brilliant lime green shoots through the soil. The juxtaposition of colors was breathtaking and seemed to symbolize the beautiful end of my old life and the fertile beginning of the monastic new.

Although I left the monastery five years later and retraced my farewell tour, I didn't hop another train for fourteen years. I was a *home guard,* that's hobo for someone who has quit riding the rails. But in the summer of 1997, I *caught out* from Glenwood Springs, Colorado. I wanted to see what had changed in the intervening thirteen years — besides the demise of the caboose. I also wanted to get some inspiration for this book. And my wife was out of town.

Glenwood Springs is not a crew change point, so there is no guarantee that the trains will stop there. I spent the entire evening waiting on the platform of a sidetracked grain car waiting in the rain. The only train that came through was moving too fast to jump. At dawn, I went back to our tiny apartment and got some sleep. Later in the day, I walked back to the yard in west Glenwood. As I was nearing it, a train pulling empty coal cars came through slowly and finally stopped. I got on the back of a car, which only had metal beams for bracing — no platform. This meant I would have to ride virtually on top of the rear wheels. If I fell asleep, I could roll off the beam to my death. I knew, however, that the train would stop in Grand Junction, Colorado — only a couple of hours away. I could easily make it that far. I sat on the center beam with my backpack behind me as a cushion. My feet were resting on the coupling and I held on to two beams on either side of me. It was much like riding a chopper. "Hallelujah, hopping again!" When the train stopped in Parachute, Colorado, I climbed into the third *unit* and rode in style.

I learned from a Grand Junction yardman that another train would not leave for over six hours. I walked to the bus station, but the daily Greyhound buses had left earlier for my destination in Salt Lake City. As I left the bus station, an Amtrak train eased by under US Highway 50, so I hustled to the depot — just in time to get a ticket to Green River, Utah.

I reveled in the contrast between my two train experiences. When someone complained at dinner about the rough ride, I offered some perspective. I walked through Green River and spent the night sleeping under a fruit stand. I hitchhiked to Salt Lake City the next day. I had a long wait, but I got there in one ride. The driver gave me the sad news that I would not get into Mormon "celestial" heaven. I was content, however, because I would probably get into the next lower "terrestrial" heaven. If it was anything like the difference between my passenger train ride and my freight train ride, it was OK with me. And I think I would prefer the company.

"   ll Roads Lead to Britt" is this Iowa town's slogan (don't tell
    A   Rome). During the annual Hobo Convention held in this north
    central community, it just might be true. There are other hobo
celebrations, but Britt's is the oldest and best known. The first convention
held in Britt was in 1900, but the gatherings started much earlier according
to the website www.hobo.com.

In the mid-1800s, hobos were repeatedly kicked out of towns and off of
trains because of strict enforcement of vagrancy laws. But members of a
union were granted free passage on most railroads and were not persecuted
for vagrancy. A few hobos in Ohio drew up articles of incorporation for a
union that any hobo nationwide could join. There were sixty-three hobos
present at the original meeting, so the group chose the name Tourist Union
#63. The railroads feared that the Tourists were a new socialist group, but
all they wanted was protection from vagrancy laws, and the freedom to look
for work. The website article claimed that some of the members of Tourist
Union #63 helped form the American Civil Liberties Union, which got
vagrancy laws repealed nationwide.

Each year Tourist Union #63 held a National Hobo Convention to renew
friendships, collect annual dues, sign up new members, and choose a
King, Queen, Crown Prince, Crown Princess, and Grand Head Pipe. The
convention was held in Danville, Illinois in 1899. Two Britt men, Thomas
A. Way and T. A. Potter, read an article about it in a Chicago paper and
wrote "Grand Head Pipe" Charles Noe. They paid Noe's way to Britt, wined
and dined him, and assured Noe that a Britt convention would be a rousing
success. It was indeed. The Britt newspaper reported: "All day on Tuesday,
the society tramps, and the genuine hobos came straggling in . . . the latter
were taken to the fair grounds where they were given nice quarters in the hog
and cattle pens and where they spent two days in perfect luxury." A hobo
foot race took place with prizes offered like: one bottle of hunyard water,
one ticket *on the cushions* (on the passenger train) from Hayfield to Titonka,
one cake of ivory soap, photo of Phil S. Reed, and three days of paid work.
Despite the success of the first endeavor, another convention was not held
in Britt until 1933. Since then there has been one every year except during
World War II.

In July 1993, my wife-to-be and I made a nonconvention pilgrimage to
Britt in between a visit to a Trappist monastery near Dubuque, Iowa and
a rigorous climb to the high point of Iowa (at the end of a trough on a hog
farm). A hobo museum had just opened in town a year earlier in the old
Chief Theater. I did some research there and bought a t-shirt that said, "It's
a Jungle Out There!" We also went to the *Hobo Jungle* — located in a park
near the Soo Line railroad tracks — where they had recently placed an old

Milwaukee Road boxcar on rails and built a shelter house with showers and dressing rooms. I bought an indelible magic marker and added my moniker at the end of the boxcar: "Freight Train Wayne." When I returned again in August 1998, the indelible inscription had delibled. I bought another t-shirt that read, "Hobo Convention — Boxcar Wear." I stopped in October 2006 and paid my respects at the hobo section of the town cemetery. I lunched on fabulous hobo potatoes at Mary Jo's Hobo House Restaurant. Recently, a campaign to raise funds for a new hobo museum was started, but has since been suspended because of the Great Recession.

They still elect a King and Queen of the Hobos every year. To be elected you must be a "true" rail rider and pass a review by a committee of hobos. Candidates receive votes in the form of audience applause following campaign speeches. There has been fierce competition and long reigns. Scoop Shovel Scotty battled it out with Hobo Ben Benson from 1936 to 1962. The Pennsylvania Kid (who in 1967 quipped, "a hobo is a workman who . . . specializes in long layoffs") and the Hardrock Kid took off their kid gloves between 1963 and 1975. Steamtrain Maury Graham dominated between 1973 and 1981, winning five times. On the female side, Longlooker Mic holds the record with ten titles between 1970 and 1985. Boxcar Betty Link won four titles in the fifties. One year, I may run for King.

There has been controversy at some of the recent conventions. Some former kings and queens did not attend the hundredth convention because of perceived ill treatment in the past. Some speculated that the reason this special gathering had such a low turnout was because of police behavior, which included unnecessary camp sweeps, unprovoked searches, and planted undercover snitches. It's ironic since this kind of police harassment was what provided the impetus for the creation of the hobo union and subsequent conventions in the first place. Some also claimed outright fraud in the election of the Queen, when an anarchist train rider was allegedly denied her rightful crown. Disaffected hobos decided to boycott Britt. Some townspeople even suggested that they avoid troublesome hobos and hire actors to portray hobo clowns.

Trampfest 2000, held in St. Paul, Minnesota, was created as an alternative hobo convention. Its rationale was laid out in a zine called *Hobocore*, "so why not move the 'real' hobo convention and free it from Britt's fat tourists, sleazy money-grubbing small-town politicians, self-satisfied right-wing politics, stupid small-minded hypocrisy, missionaries, cops, and RV-driving fake hobos?" One day I may run for King at Trampfest, too, on the Anti-Hyphen Hobo Unity ticket.

Do all roads lead to Britt? No, but all souls do get back to God. It takes more than one lifetime, but there is no eternal damnation. Our finite actions cannot cause such an infinite reaction. A loving God cannot create an everlasting hell. We create temporary hells when we misuse our free will.

Minturn, Colorado is an eclectic oddity — a blue-collar oasis nestled between upscale Vail and Beaver Creek ski resorts. The Vail Valley epitomizes many things I dislike as an environmentalist and city planner. Imagine my surprise when I discovered nearby Minturn, population one thousand. Minturn had maintained its town character despite intense development pressures. Its large rail yard was one of its distinguishing features. Crew changes took place there and *helper* engines were added to get trains to the top of Tennessee Pass. The mine at nearby Gilman, which closed in 1977, attracted a large number of New Mexicans of Hispanic descent, who add to Minturn's colorful culture. An unusual geologic formation, Lion's Head rock, guards the town. The town logo features a rendering of the nearby Mount of the Holy Cross, a fourteen-thousand-foot mountain with a snow cross on its face. I climbed it once while living in Colorado.

Mountain men and fur trappers came through this confluence of Gore Creek and the Eagle River in the 1830s. The Ute and the Arapahoe Indians fought over the area on Battle Mountain in 1849, and the gold seekers came after 1858. Minturn was created in 1887 when the Denver and Rio Grande Railroad (D&RG) arrived. General William Jackson Palmer started the D&RG in 1870 with the intention of connecting Denver with Mexico City. He lost a race (more like a war) to Raton Pass, at the New Mexico border, to the Santa Fe Railroad, but was awarded the right-of-way to the lucrative mining operations to the west through Royal Gorge.

The D&RG line was the highest main line railroad in the country and their motto was "through the Rockies, not around them." It pushed to Leadville, then over 10,240 foot Tennessee Pass to the mines in Gilman and Red Cliff, in 1880. In 1887, the rail lines were extended to the town that was first called Kingston, then Booco's Station, then Minturn. Renamed for Robert B. Minturn, a shipping millionaire responsible for raising the money to bring the rails west, it was incorporated in 1904 on land donated by George G. Booco. In 1942, Camp Hale was constructed above Minturn as a training facility for the famed Tenth Mountain Division.

In 1994, Minturn advertised for a Town Manager. I was so enamored by the town that I applied, even though I had not been in the business for thirteen years. I did extensive research on the town, and had a long conversation at the Turntable Restaurant with a man who served as mayor of Minturn for twenty years. The Turntable Restaurant is a classic diner where train crews from adjoining dormitory rooms, townspeople, and tourists once ate while model trains ran on overhead tracks.

Fortunately, I did not get the Minturn job because, in a few years, Minturn's character was severely compromised with the development of seven out-of-character four-plexes along the Eagle River. The Union Pacific (UP) absorbed the D&RG and in 1997 they stopped using the route through Minturn (before I got to hop it). The rail worker's dormitory was turned into a motel and Vail Associates sued Minturn to acquire some of their underused water rights.

I half-jokingly considered running yuppie freight hopping tours from Minturn to Tennessee Pass, complete with Mulligan Stew at a makeshift *hobo jungle*. Since modern males no longer have rituals that help them transition into manhood, I figured I could capitalize on this need and offer to make them official "Hobo Sapiens" with their manliness assured once they completed the ride. I would have gotten my excursions listed in "The Sixty Things a Man Must Do in His Life" in *Men's Journal*. I even planned a website, www.imgullabull.com. (A rival of P. T. Barnum said, "There's a sucker born every minute." But now there are millions of suckers born for every minute of television advertising.)

I would have told my charges what was needed to successfully hop a freight train, such as: 1) a clue. If they had common sense, I would not let them hop. Common sense is the greatest oxymoron of them all. Boxcars full of uncommonly good sense are needed; 2) bail. Riding the rails is trespassing. Jail is possible; 3) a fake, henna tattoo that features the letters "FTRA." This stands for the Freight Train Riders of America, the supposed *hobo mafia*; and 4) a note of permission from their personal growth advisor.

I would teach them: 1) to pack garbage bags for raingear — none of that fancy Gore-Tex stuff; 2) cheap wine etiquette: the bottle must have a twist top; Red Ripple goes with beef jerky; White Ripple with sardines; 3) to avoid wearing designer jeans. Can you Guess how big their Gap would be if the FTRA caught them wearing those fancy pants? And finally; 4) I would explain how freight train hopping would make them feel — exhilarated for the first fifteen minutes, miserable for the rest of the trip. After the trip, they'd strut like they'd hit a home run in Little League, because they would have become a man — unless, of course, they *caught the westbound* instead and became a dead man.

The Turntable Restaurant in Minturn reminded me of the Dandylion Café in Phoenix, where I got a job washing dishes in 1970. The owner was a large, gruff woman from New York. One day someone telephoned to inquire about the daily special and asked if it was any good. Big mistake. Maggie bellowed, "If it weren't any good, it wouldn't be on the damned menu." She slammed down the phone and muttered, "Idiots." Meditation is like Maggie's special. If it weren't any good, it wouldn't be on the menu of almost every mystic path. Plus, the price is right.

CHAPTER 25: FOAMER

A freight train horn echoing through the spectacular Glenwood Canyon in Colorado is pure joy to my ears. A freight train horn on a stationary engine stuck in the "on" position in the early morning is an alarm clock from hell. That's what I woke up to one silvery morning in Glenwood Springs.

After first swatting my alarm clock in a brain fog, I deduced the source of the annoyance. Surely they will turn it off I thought at 7:04 and 7:10 and 7:13 and 7:21 and 7:25 and 7:33. Finally, my curiosity and my aggravation badgered me to get up, get dressed and investigate.

I drove down Midland Avenue past Red Mountain and discovered the source of the fingers-on-a-chalkboard screeching. The horn on a *helper* engine in the middle of a coal train was the auditory offender. I turned on Devereux Road and went to the yard entrance by the Coors distribution warehouse. By then the horn had been mercifully shut off. A man was standing nearby, so I parked my car and walked up to him.

"They finally got that horn shut off."

"I had to do it manually."

"Who are you?"

"The hogshead."

"The what?"

"The engineer."

"You going to stop here long?"

"A couple of hours. The crew is going to the Village Inn for breakfast. I'm waiting for a yardman to pick me up."

A Union Pacific truck pulled up. As the hogshead got in, someone asked him whom I was.

"Just a foamer."

They drove off and left me wanting to know what my moniker meant. I motored to the Village Inn, went up to their table and asked if I could join them. The three of them — the hogshead, the conductor and a conductor-in-training — said it was fine. They were impressed when I told them the origins of the term *hobo*. We had a pleasant conversation filled with railroad gossip.

There is a story about a church that had a vicious gossip. One Sunday, she confronted a man who had just started attending services. She walked up to him and declared, "We saw your truck in front of the tavern and we know what you were doing there!" The man left the building without saying a word. But later that day, he parked his truck in front of the woman's house and simply left it there overnight.

Before my visit with the train crew ended, I finally asked the question I was dying to have answered.

"What is a foamer?"

"Foamers are you fanatics who foam at the mouth over everything railroad-related."

I was a founding member of the Western Colorado Chapter of the National Railway Historical Society. I joined primarily seeking inspiration to finish this book, because I am more hobo than railfan. Most railfans frown on freight train hopping. Some are even being recruited by railroads out West to act as eyes for the railroad police. Still, I ended up serving as chapter treasurer and gained greater appreciation for railroad history and preservation. I also gave two talks about Alaska railroads — the White Pass and Yukon Route and the Copper River and Northwest Railroad — which have morphed into chapters in this book. The group adopted the name I suggested for our chapter newsletter — "The Foamer." The motto I suggested for our group followed the same line of thinking — "Rabid for Rail."

Religions have their fair share of foamers. I believe that all the major religions are like spokes on a wheel leading to the same hub (God). Each of the spiritual spokes has levels of progression as it nears the hub — from the barbarian, to the fundamentalist, to the atheist, to the spiritual, to the mystic and finally, to oneness with the hub (see Appendix B, page 110). The belief-based foamer near the outer rim says, "My God can beat up your God," and calls those of other faiths "heathen, heathen, heathen." But to the mystic nearing Oneness, it's "buddy, buddy, buddy."

Star Wars. That's what popped into my mind when I saw a hundred lights blazing on a piece of machinery that I had never seen before. It was in the Glenwood Springs, Colorado rail yard. I went to find out if aliens had landed.

I drove along the Colorado River and parked at the Coca Cola plant near the yard entrance. The closer I got to the ship, the odder it seemed. I was half expecting some "War of the Worlds" creature to raise its head and vaporize me, but I made my way right up to the craft unharmed. I spied what appeared to be a humanoid at work on the deck. I approached and asked about his contraption. He told me that it was a rail grinder complete with support cars that acted like a rolling mechanic's shop. They were grinding the track through Glenwood Canyon.

When I asked him what was wrong with it, he replied, "Track can have lots of problems like shelling, spalling, side wear, plastic flow, dipped welds, corrugation, fatigue. I'm not sure what the problem is here. I just maintain this beast at night. The rest of the crew does the grinding during the day between freight trains."

They had just deadheaded in from a job in California. (In November 2006, a similar maintenance train became a runaway and derailed in the mountains east of Sacramento — killing two members of the crew.) The crewmembers were from all over the country, he said. They were often away from home for weeks at a time. All but one of them was single. The married guy had just gotten laid off from another job and was desperate for work.

I inquired about grinding speed. He answered, "We can only go a couple of miles per hour here. This is corrective grinding. It takes longer. If you do preventative grinding on a regular basis, it takes less time and triples the life of the track. Track is the most valuable asset a railroad owns. It pays to keep it up. Badly maintained track can cause a train to derail, shortens rail life, causes poorer gas mileage and slows train speeds. Curved track has the most problems. The wheel and the track are supposed to have a certain shape. After they've been over each other enough, the wheel starts taking the shape of the track and the track starts taking the shape of the wheel."

Like husband and wife, I thought.

When I asked about fires, he told me that the grinders have a fire suppression system, but they still have to be on their toes. They let the local fire departments know of their plans, just in case they need back up. Loram, a company out of Minnesota, manufactured the machine. He said that there were cheaper outfits — grinders can have between four and ninety-six grinding stones — but the smaller models took a lot longer to grind the track.

When I told him I was a part-time hobo, he added, "Grinding is good for you, too. It makes for a smoother ride."

The next day, I had to drive through Glenwood Canyon on my way to Denver. The acrid smell that filled my nostrils told me that I was near the grinder. I slowed my car to watch the process, but I was on the freeway so I couldn't dally long. Down the road, I saw a train on a sidetrack waiting for the grinding operation to stop temporarily so it could pass. I've twice seen track grinders on sidetracks in Norman, Oklahoma since then. I'm glad to know that they are keeping the rails safe for riders like me.

I drove away thinking that my spiritual life is a lot like a track's life. As track is the most important asset of a railroad, so is my spiritual life imperative to me. If I do preventive maintenance by meditating daily, my ride in life goes more smoothly. If I neglect my meditation routine or meditate poorly, my life is apt to derail, or at best need serious corrective measures. It pays to be a grind.

There were about fifty railroad ventures proposed in Alaska, but only nine became operational. The White Pass & Yukon Route (WP&Y) was the first. In June 2000, I rode the railroad from Skagway, Alaska to Fraser, British Columbia, Canada, took a bus to Whitehorse in Yukon Territory, and hitchhiked four hundred miles of the Alaska Highway. I took the fantastic, funky Alaska Marine Highway ferry up the Inland Passage from Bellingham, Washington to Skagway, Alaska. Skagway seemed like a movie set, spruced up for the centennial of both the railroad and the town.

Freight operations on the narrow gauge railroad ceased in 1982, so my only option was the passenger train. Passengers like me, who were going on to Whitehorse, were put on the same car — separating us from cruise ship passengers. I bonded with several people who I ran into throughout Alaska on the remainder of my trip. I had promised my local National Railway Historical Society chapter that I would give a talk on the WP&Y, so I took slides of the shop area and the ride over White Pass. I interspersed that later lecture with verses from Bill Stains' haunting tune "Sourdough."

The WP&Y was constructed as a result of the Klondike Gold Rush. There had been earlier, smaller Yukon River gold strikes, and at the time there were an estimated ten thousand people in the area "placer mining." In August 1896, "Lying George" Carmack and Native Americans Skookum Jim and Dawson Charlie found "color" on the Klondike River — a tributary of the Yukon River. After they filed their claim, several thousand miners, only a few hundred miles downstream, raced to the Klondike and staked out every square inch of it. It was the richest placer stream ever found in the world. The real gold rush was over and the fool's gold rush had begun.

In July 1897, boats landed in Seattle and San Francisco laden with tons of gold. Word spread like marmalade across recession-ravaged America. Roughly a hundred thousand "stampeders" migrated north. At most forty thousand completed the backbreaking, yearlong trek to newly incorporated Dawson City on the Klondike River. Most took ships out of Seattle to either Skagway or nearby rival Dyea, Alaska at the end of the Inland Passage. Dyea was the starting point for those hiking over brutal Chilkoot Pass. They had to hike the "meanest thirty-three miles" and scale the last "icy steps to hell" twenty-five to forty times in roughly a three-month span carrying the ton of supplies that the Mounties at the Canadian border required of each entrant. Roughly thirty thousand did so. One man even carried a piano. Photos of stampeders going ant-like up the final, grueling grade are icons of the Klondike Gold Rush. Once they reached the headwaters of the Yukon River in British Columbia, they had to whipsaw boards to build boats to float down the dangerous, rapids-filled stream. In the spring of 1898, over seven thousand boats made the six hundred-mile float trip.

A longer, but less steep route went out of Skagway over White Pass, which was falsely promoted as an all-weather route. Skagway was named after the Tlingit word meaning "windy place." It grew to approximately fifteen thousand opportunists during the Gold Rush and became the first incorporated city in Alaska. First the stampeders had to negotiate the "windy" merchants and the slippery scam artists. Packhorses could be used on this trail, but three thousand were killed trying it. By September 1897, the route was destroyed by overuse. When comparing the two trails, one stampeder said, "It didn't matter which one you took, you'd wished you had taken the other."

In came the railroad. British-financed civil engineer E. C. Hawkins and Canadian railroad contractor "Big Mike" Heney met by accident in a Skagway hotel and in April 1898 the WP&Y was organized. With American engineering and thirty thousand brave laborers the task was begun. A second-hand Baldwin engine, imported from the Columbia and Puget Sound Railway, chugged up the four miles of track that had been laid by July 1898, making it the northernmost railroad in the Western Hemisphere. They reached White Pass in February 1899. Another crew was laying track from Whitehorse and they met at Carcross, British Columbia, Canada where the Golden Spike was driven in July 1900. It took two years, two months, two days, two hours, two minutes, and two seconds to finish the task. By then the Klondike Gold Rush had peaked and many moved on to the next big strike in Nome, Alaska.

The building of the 110-mile WP&Y was an engineering marvel. In 1994, it was declared an International Historic Civil Engineering Landmark — along with the Eiffel Tower, the Statue of Liberty, and the Panama Canal. During World War II, the WP&Y was the chief, round-the-clock supplier for the U. S. Army's construction of the crucial Alaska Highway. In the 1960s, lead and zinc were discovered north of Whitehorse and the WP&YR was reconstructed to handle that traffic with new diesel electric locomotives. After the major mine shut down in 1982, the WP&Y was forced to follow suit. It reopened in 1988 exclusively for tourist trains.

Much more money was made off the fools who rushed north than was ever made prospecting for Klondike gold. Most stampeders became laborers in other men's mines. Only about one out of ten men who made the journey north struck it rich. And only a handful of those kept their hard-earned dollars. Many who became rich died unhappy. That is the way of material desires.

Non-spiritual desire is our greatest enemy on the mystic path. As long as we have earthly desires we will be forced to reincarnate — fettered to the wheel of misfortune — because according to karmic law all desires must be fulfilled. They are like poisoned honey — tasty initially, but problem-laden. When an elderly woman named Hope was repeatedly asked to go outside, she finally said, "All right, I'll put my shoes on, but I won't put my teeth in." We have to put our shoes on and our teeth in and bite the bullet of virtue and compassion, which may taste bitter at first, but leads to lasting satisfaction.

🚂 CHAPTER 28: FUEL FOR THOUGHT 🚂

M y foray to Alaska in 2000 involved most forms of transportation in existence. Five modes stand out. I have already mentioned three: 1) the Alaska Marine Highway ferry up the Inside Passage; 2) the White Pass and Yukon Route train ride; and 3) hitchhiking the Alaska Highway from Whitehorse to Tok, Alaska. The fourth method was a bush plane flight from Homer to Seldovia, Alaska. The fifth adventure was a freight train ride on the Alaska Railroad (ARR) from Fairbanks to Healy, Alaska.

The Alaska Railroad began in 1914, when the United States Government bought several failed railroads. Colonel Frederick Mears, who oversaw the relocation of the Panama Canal Railroad, supervised the railroad's construction using discarded equipment from the Panama Canal endeavor. Their headquarters was set up on Ship Creek, which later became the city of Anchorage. In July 1923, President Warren Harding drove the Golden Spike near the town of Nenana, completing the railroad. During World War II, The American military built a top-secret port in Whittier, Alaska and tunneled through a mountain to connect to the main line tracks south of Anchorage. That way, if the Japanese bombed the only other deep-water port in Seward, the military could still ship supplies by rail on this alternative route. In 1985, the State of Alaska purchased the line from the federal government.

After telephoning the Alaska Railroad and blarneying my way into a man's confidence, I found out the location of their yard in Fairbanks. One afternoon, while I was doing laundry at a friend's home, my intuition told me that it was time to *catch out*. My host was a bit confused by my behavior. Why was I leaving in the afternoon when the passenger trains always left in the morning? Why didn't I want to go to the passenger train depot?

When we were getting off the Johansen Expressway, I spotted the rows of railcars that I was certain would soon be heading to Anchorage. There was even a caboose on the end. It was a welcome sight, since cabooses had been eliminated from trains in the Lower 48. My friend wanted to drop me off at the yard office — a place where I didn't want to be seen. She didn't understand the illegal nature of my endeavor. We finally said our good-byes and I went to inspect the train. The cars were nearly all tankers and experience told me they were probably full of motor oil. I later learned that they contained jet fuel — the stuff that burned the Twin Towers on September 11th.

Tankers are not particularly ridable, but luckily there was one lumber car, flat with high end walls, that was right next to the caboose. I found a hidden niche on my alloyed steed and melded with the freight. I was energized when the engines drove up, assembled the four strings of cars, charged the brakes with air, and galloped down the line. After three hours of taiga trees and chit chat with steel, we sidetracked where the Rocky Mountains end and grizzlies roust the spring. To my delight, the crew changed in Healy, which was only a few miles from my destination — Denali National Park.

Later, while riding a passenger train from Seward to Anchorage, I learned from a conductor that the Alaska Railroad had tried to eliminate the cabooses — just like in the Lower 48 — but it proved too costly. In the States almost all of the switches are changed electronically from panels in master control rooms, for example BNSF's is in Fort Worth, Texas and the UP's is in Omaha, Nebraska. In Alaska, they had to be switched manually. That meant the conductor in the engine had to get out, move the switch, wait until the train pulled forward, and put the switch back in its original position. The employee then had to walk the entire length of the train back to the engine. The resulting dead time proved to be too expensive. The conductor claimed that they went back to cabooses so the workers in the back of the train could make the final switch.

Unfortunately, cabooses had been eliminated from the ARR when I returned to Alaska in 2003 to drive tour buses in Denali National Park. I heard another version of the story when I rode a passenger train from Anchorage to Whittier to catch the ferry to Cordova, Alaska. The conductor on that ride told me that the cabooses I saw in 2000 had been added after a train wreck that happened the previous December. Three locomotives and fifteen tanker cars — full of jet fuel — derailed. Four of the tankers leaked about a hundred thousand gallons of their volatile contents near Talkeetna (the town that inspired the "Northern Exposure" television show). The spill occurred only about a thousand feet from the Big Susitna River in an area inaccessible by road. The Talkeetna spill came on the heels of a smaller spill that occurred in October when the daily fuel train from North Pole, Alaska also derailed. It cost the railroad twelve million dollars to clean up the spills, causing them to operate in the red for that year. Cabooses were revived as a "permanent" safety measure. The "permanent" safety measure lasted until the general manager of the railroad was replaced. The new CEO promptly eliminated them again.

Had I known in 2000 that the tankers contained jet fuel and not motor oil I probably would not have hopped that train. I'm glad I didn't know. That may be why God usually gives us the minimum amount of information needed to make our next step in life. If we knew more, we would surely balk.

The Vikings may have gotten to Heavener, Oklahoma's Prairie of the Long Grass long before my wife and I did. There is strong evidence of a Scandinavian settlement in Newfoundland, Canada many years before Columbus "discovered" America. (It's too bad the Native Americans didn't think to discover it.) Some also believe that the Vikings continued down the East Coast, around Florida, into the Gulf of Mexico, and up the Mississippi River and its tributaries. The Heavener Runestone, a property marker allegedly left by Viking explorers between 600 and 900 A.D., is lasting evidence of these travels. And being of Norwegian descent, I wanted to see it.

In April 2002, my wife and I traveled the Talimena Scenic Byway in eastern Oklahoma. We got off the byway near dusk, headed north on Highway 259, and made our way to Heavener to scout out a motel. I had an ulterior motive in choosing Heavener as our overnight destination. I knew that the Kansas City Southern Railroad, the town's largest employer, changed crews there and I wanted to explore their yard. It would be an easy place to *catch out*, although certainly not on a trip with my wife.

It was dark when we arrived in Heavener. Road signs told us that a right turn would lead downtown. A boxcar (with attached deer pens), which serves as their Chamber of Commerce, was our pivot point. We crossed four sets of tracks and were met by the Stanley and Bill buildings, which happen to be our father's names. We cruised downtown, which featured four Mexican restaurants. One two-story brick building was painted bright purple. We later found out that outraged locals were attempting to create a historic district in downtown Heavener to prevent such future abuse of brick. The town also sported a twenty-four hour diner to accommodate railroad employees who work late shifts.

I made a wrong turn that dead-ended at the freight yard by the engine house. We doubled back to look for lodging and discovered the Crane Motel. While it met my local color standards, my wife would have preferred something nicer (I wanted to camp, so it was a compromise). I did my evening meditation, which was interspersed with familiar railroad sounds. The motel, it turned out, was right next to the northern end of the yard. I drank too much coffee that day so, after my meditation, I was still wide-awake. To work off some caffeine, I told my wife that I was going to explore the yards. After promising her that I would not actually hop a freight train, I couldn't resist casing the yard just to figure out how I might do so in the future.

Next to the yard office, three engines sat ready to pull a string of cars to Shreveport, Louisiana. Easy pickings, but I restrained myself. Later that evening, a train with only two engines (which usually means it is a work train) left the yard. It looked like it was headed toward Kansas City,

Missouri, but work trains can veer off to places you don't want to go. I did not hop that one either. I went back to our room, where my wife was waiting up for me. I do keep my word. But . . . I did not promise that I would not hop a train out of or into this town another time.

From Heavener, the northbound trains go through Poteau, Sallisaw and Stilwell, Oklahoma. (Stilwell is named for the founder of the Kansas City Southern Railroad, Arthur Stilwell.) The trains cross the state line and proceed through the Ozark Plateau towns of Siloam Springs and Gravette, Arkansas before entering Missouri. They traverse Neosho and Joplin before veering into Kansas where they change crews again in Pittsburg.

The Kansas City Southern website, www.kcsi.com, was not particularly useful, but it had a link to the Kansas City Southern Historic Society website, www.kcshs.org, which featured some helpful information. As it turns out, a northbound train usually arrives in Heavener about 2:30 p.m., presumably adds other cars, and leaves again at midnight, heading toward Kansas City. It is a *manifest train*, which means it has a mix of freight cars as opposed to a *unit train* where all the cars are the same. The Internet has certainly made freight hopping easier.

With a little legwork and some web browsing, I developed a plan. It looked like this: 1) take a Greyhound bus to Sallisaw, Oklahoma; 2) hitch to Heavener; catch the train north and try to get off in Joplin, Missouri; and 3) take the bus back to Norman, Oklahoma. There is no guarantee, however, that the train would stop in Joplin. If not, I'd have to travel to Pittsburg, Kansas, where they change crews again, and cobble together another way home. A second option would be to drive to Heavener and ride trains to Pittsburg and back.

Simple plans, but do you remember what happens to us when we plan? God guffaws. Oscar Wilde said something similar, "When the gods wish to punish us, they answers our prayers."

C *atching out* in smaller, quaint towns is a mellower experience when compared to navigating big city yards. Chickasha, Oklahoma is such a place and has a colorful past. The Union Pacific Railroad absorbed the Chicago, Rock Island, and Pacific Railroad (CRI&P) and its line from Wichita, Kansas to Fort Worth, Texas, but Chickasha was still a crew change point in January 2003. I drove over from Norman, Oklahoma to inspect the yard prior to taking a future free ride. Coming into town from the east on Oklahoma Highway 9, I crossed the main track via an overpass. On the other side of the bridge, the old depot building, built in 1914 and renovated in 1998, is clearly visible. I parked on Chickasha Avenue and walked east toward the railroad tracks. I veered south along First Street until I found an easy way to cut through to the rail yard. I passed an abandoned metal warehouse that was obviously a *hobo jungle* at one time. The area held the Guinness World Record for the most empty Sunnybrook Whiskey bottles. An acrid odor emanated from the now burned out building.

Chickasha came into being when the CRI&P laid track across Oklahoma Territory to Houston, Texas along the old Chisholm Trail, famous for cattle drives. A dubious business called "Rock Island Camp" followed the railroad's construction. In 1892, when the Rock Island Railroad stopped laying track for several months, Chickasha emerged as a small shack town. Located within the Chickasaw Indian Nation, the railroad named the town after the tribe. The spelling evolved over time.

In October 1897, Al Jennings and his gang held up a train just north of town. Jennings's men robbed the passengers, but could not blow open the safe. After two failed attempts, they left with a bag of registered letters, a keg of whiskey and a stalk of bananas. They no doubt took the bananas so they could throw the peels behind them, causing the pursuing posse to slip. Two famous lawmen, Bill Tilghman and Heck Thomas, rode down on a special train to hunt the outlaws. Jennings was caught, tried, and sent to prison in Ohio. He only served a few years because of legal technicalities and President Teddy Roosevelt eventually pardoned him. Jennings had been a lawyer before he turned against the law. He ran for Governor in 1914, and finished his days on a chicken farm in California — a natural progression from lawyer to convict to politician to chicken plucker.

In October 1915, there was a head-on train wreck similar to the one that made Casey Jones famous. In this case, a freight train was instructed to pull off on a sidetrack near Agawam, just south of Chickasha, but the orders got scrambled. Instead, it headed straight for a passenger train controlled by engineer Norman Brooks, who held the honor of driving the first train from Chickasha to Fort Worth, Texas. Brooks died heroically trying to brake the train and cut the steam instead of *joining the birds* by jumping to safety as his fireman urged.

At one time, Chickasha was a divisional railroad terminal with a roundhouse and large repair facilities. However, when the rail workers voted to join a nationwide strike, the president of the Rock Island said he would, "reduce Chickasha to a one horse town." He made good on that threat by moving the rail yards to El Reno, Oklahoma, which took jobs and taxes away from this Washita River Valley town. Perhaps a little old-fashioned Oklahoma anarchy would have proven useful.

In his book *Progressive Oklahoma*, Danney Goble reports that railroads in the West practiced corporate extortion. Towns were forced to pay exorbitant bounties to get tracks run through their jurisdictions, and railroads often acted as masters rather than servants. Before the Cherokee Outlet Land Run of 1893, the Rock Island Railroad built a trunk line to El Reno, Oklahoma and established two depots to the north, Enid Station and Pond Creek Station. The Federal Government designated both depots as county seats.

The railroad then conspired to secretly purchase key parcels of property before the Land Run. The Interior Department thwarted their plans by moving both county seats three miles to the south. But the railroad refused to stop or even slow down through these fledgling towns. A territorial suit to force the railroad to do so was thrown out on a technicality in 1894. One day later, trestle supports were sawn through and a simultaneous dynamite blast twisted tracks. A judge dismissed the case against the arrested leaders of the revolt. Congress soon passed legislation that said *any* railroad passing through *any* county seat had to provide depot facilities. No mention of the Oklahoma incident was made, but it seemed clear that Oklahoma anarchy led to the humbling of the mighty fine Rock Island Line.

I continued up the tracks that day until I got to the Union Pacific yard office on North 4th Street. I went inside and confirmed that Chickasha was still a crew change point, since these things do change. I walked back to my car and drove south until I reached Ada Sipuel Avenue. In 1947, Ada Sipuel Fisher successfully sued the University of Oklahoma Law School when state law forbade them to admit her because she was black. I turned east on the avenue named for her and drove until I came to the main line track again. Two trains were stopped on separate tracks facing each other like blacks facing off against whites. They were just far enough back from the crossing so that the warning lights were not triggered. I drove between them like Krishna drove Arjuna between armies before the battle of Kurukshetra in the Bhagavad-Gita. That battle is symbolic of the daily battle for freedom waged by our souls against our egos. It's also similar to that battle for justice that Ada Sipuel Fisher triggered against Oklahoma prejudice.

▄▀ CHAPTER 31: RULING GRADES ▀▄▄

Ifinally *caught out* on a Kansas City Southern (KCS) freight train in Pittsburg, Kansas. In October 2003, I had thoroughly checked out this town on a return trip from Minnesota. I got into town in the wee hours and napped in my car in Schlanger Park. The park was next to the tracks and — soon after I arrived — a northbound train drove by, stopped, and released its air brakes. I followed the tracks northward to find the yard, which is located at 23rd Street. I explored more of Pittsburg, had lunch at Harry's Café, toured the historic Stilwell Hotel, and headed home.

The Stilwell Hotel was named after Arthur Stilwell, the founder of the KCS. He learned about railroading from his grandfather, Hamblin Stilwell, one of the founders of the New York Central Railroad and builder of the Erie Canal. Unlike other railroads, the KCS was built after the Midwest was settled. Observing that it was fourteen hundred miles from Kansas City to the Atlantic Ocean and only eight hundred miles to the Gulf of Mexico, Stilwell realized he could reduce shipping distances by more than one-third by heading south instead of east. He started by incorporating the Kansas City Suburban Belt Line Railroad in 1887 and later purchased two other railroads, which gave him track as far as Sulphur Springs, Arkansas.

The financial panic of 1893 hampered railroad building, so Stilwell went to Holland (where his flour was to be shipped), and sold stock. In gratitude, many of the towns along the line are named after prominent Dutch investors, including DeRidder, Louisiana, where my wife's parents once lived. While other railroads went bankrupt, Stilwell's rolled on. In 1896, Stilwell signed contracts for over two million dollars worth of new equipment to be paid for by a bond. But the Dutch investors said they would only buy the bonds if McKinley won the 1896 Presidential election. In desperation, Stilwell went to his friend, George Pullman. Stilwell's grandfather had given Pullman his start driving the mules used to pull barges on the Erie Canal. Stilwell's connection paid off when Pullman and other investors loaned him the funds needed to avert the crisis.

Stilwell could have purchased a railroad going to Galveston, Texas, but wisely decided to build an inland city called Port Arthur on Lake Sabine, out of harms way from hurricanes. He commissioned a canal to be dug from the Lake to the Gulf. The last spike was driven just north of Beaumont, Texas in 1897. Stilwell soon became desperate for *rolling stock*, wheeled vehicles used by a railroad, and again his friend Pullman came to his rescue with a loan of three million dollars. The cars were ordered but, before Stilwell could get Pullman's signature on the necessary papers, Pullman died. The railroad went into receivership and was reorganized as the Kansas City Southern Railway in 1900. Stilwell moved on and started another railroad that occupied his time until his death in 1928. After Stilwell's departure, the world's first oil well gusher was struck in 1901 in Beaumont, Texas and the KCS had the boon it needed to get it out of fiscal trouble.

Franklin Playter, who founded Pittsburg, Kansas, was a friend of Stilwell and enticed him to swing his tracks into Kansas by building the Stilwell Hotel in 1889 and offering him free easements. In 1893, the railroad arrived in Pittsburg, a city built on its coalmines and smelting operations. Today, Pittsburg is home to Pittsburg State University, whose mascot is a gorilla. I find this to be ironic since the area is one of the hotbeds of the anti-evolution movement. Are they, too, "going to the apes?" Albert Einstein understood the dance between science and religion. He said, "Science without religion is lame. Religion without science is blind."

The KCS was the only major railroad west of the Mississippi that I had not hopped yet and I always loved the Byrd's version of the song, "Kansas City Southern." In 2006 when the opportunity presented itself, I jumped at the chance. My brother Ron and I had met in Texas to drive our parents' van back to Minnesota that spring. On our way north, we stopped in Norman, Oklahoma, where I picked up my car and my brother followed me in the van to Sallisaw, Oklahoma. I left my vehicle in that town and, together in the van again, we continued on to Pittsburg, Kansas. We spent the night in the Holiday Lodge, a short distance from the railroad yard.

The next morning, I said farewell to my sibling and walked toward the humming yard. A coal train was waiting under a new overpass. I hid between the first two coal cars and, when a crew change took place and no one was in the front engine to see me, I snuck into the third *unit*. I rode through the Ozark Plateau in grand style. We crossed into Arkansas just after 11:00 a.m. and chugged up the *ruling grade,* the steepest grade for a train.

The train was going too fast for me to jump off safely in Sallisaw, so I had to go all the way to Heavener, Oklahoma. The train stopped at a fueling station on the north end of town. I hopped off and walked a few hundred feet to Highway 59, stuck out my thumb and ten minutes later had a ride from a student from Brazil to my car in Sallisaw. I explored the sleepy little town, had a bite to eat at Dora's Café, picked up a hitchhiker to even out my karma and headed home recharged.

Trains are given enough engines to just barely creep up *ruling grades*. Our lives also come upon such *ruling grades*. God gives us just enough power to make it up them: this is how God teaches us to stretch and grow. As Helen Keller said, "Character cannot be developed in ease and quiet."

Wayne with his wife, Licia, and his niece's children, Isaac and Cora

With mother-in-law, Felicia Reid

D ave Barry observed, "All of us are born with a set of instinctive fears — of falling, of the dark, of lobsters, of falling on lobsters in the dark, or speaking before a Rotary Club, and the words 'Some Assembly Required.'" Robert Frost said, "There's nothing I'm afraid of like scared people." Not wanting to be afraid of myself, I looked fear in the face on a freight train hop to Texas in 2005.

When I *caught out* to Texas, I had not hopped in the Lower 48 since 1997 and I had heard rumors that trains were much tougher to ride. There were four alleged reasons for this: 1) railroad security increased exponentially after September 11th; 2) rail inspections had expanded when police were looking for the infamous "Railroad Killer," Angel Resendez; 3) mergers between Western railroads resulted in tougher rules; and 4) the supposed *hobo mafia*, the Freight Train Riders of America, was on the loose. In addition, Texas itself had a nasty reputation for sadistic *railroad dicks*.

I had never hoboed in Texas and wanted to do so. I seriously doubted that riding the rails had become that much tougher. I suspected that the media manipulated a lot of the stories. There are just too many miles of track for railroad police to cover and too many ways to avoid them. Police might crack down after a big incident, but soon they start to slack off. Hobos now have more civil rights, so *cinder dicks* are far less likely to pummel us. Perhaps I was looking fear in the face. Perhaps I was acting out because of my disappointment that Joseph Ratzinger was named Pope in April 2005 instead of me. At any rate, if you tell me I can't, I'm likely to prove that I can.

Needless to say, my wife was not thrilled about the Texas plan. But she knows that thoughts are things and we attract whatever we think about. She also subscribes to the Unity mantra, "thoughts held in mind produce after their own kind." So she he quickly realized that surrounding me with light and positive thoughts was better than the alternative.

I thoroughly checked out the yards in Oklahoma City in order to find the best spot to hop a Burlington Northern Santa Fe (BNSF) train. I had once applied for a job transporting rail crews at their main yard on Eastern Avenue and Southeast 89th Street. I returned and explored it thoroughly, looking for places where I would not be seen from the tower. I also checked out a secondary yard further to the north, just west of the State Capitol. I looked at points in between. I decided to *catch out* where the tracks intersected Northeast 13th Street, a four lane paved crossing where the trains crept by slowly.

One morning in April, I boarded a Norman bus to Oklahoma City. Just before we exited Interstate 40 in the downtown area, I noticed a freight train on the elevated tracks next to historic Bricktown. I changed my plan, got off the bus and walked up the raised section toward the train. A *flashing rear-end device* was attached to the northernmost car, which told me the train was heading south, but I couldn't tell if any engines were coupled to it. At the crack of noon, I climbed onto the back of a grain car and waited as inconspicuously as possible. An hour later, the train pulled out. After a half-hour, it pulled into the main yard where it stopped — and sat, and sat, and sat. Two hours later, three engines pulled up on the track next to me and began to build an *intermodal train* of *piggyback* flatcars. The *units* went back and forth as they picked up strings of rail cars. When the third engine stopped right next to me on one of their passes, I made my move to mount it. Success! The train maneuvered forward and backward a few additional times and finally left the yard at 3:30 p.m.

The train was a *hotshot,* and all other trains pulled over on sidetracks to let us scream by. We meandered through the Arbuckle Mountains along the Washita River, when I saw a sight. As the river curved around a high rock outcropping, I spied dozens of majestic eagles perched in trees or hovering in the air. On the other side of the river, numerous lanky herons were wading in the rapids, looking for fish. It seems to me that this amazing juxtaposition ought to produce a moral, but I can't find it. You tell me: guess the lesson and win a prize.

The train got into Gainesville, Texas around 6:30 p.m. and I was pleasantly surprised to see them change crews. This meant that I did not have to go into the tougher BNSF yard in Fort Worth, Texas. A northbound Amtrak train was supposed to leave Gainesville at 6:41 p.m. I got off the freight and sprinted toward the train depot. I waved furiously, but the engineers ignored me and pulled out on time. Missing the train gave me a chance to do a historic walking tour of the town and have a bite to eat at Stoolies Bar and Grill. After dark, while I was looking for a place to camp, a northbound freight train pulled in and stopped to change crews. I surreptitiously climbed on the back of a grain car. The moon was nearly full. The weather was unseasonably warm. The ride was magical.

Around midnight, the train pulled onto a sidetrack in Noble, Oklahoma, just south of my home in Norman. I leaped off and started walking home. Looking suspicious toting a backpack at that late hour, one of Noble's finest pulled up, asked for my ID and ran a computer check on me. After he found that I had a clean record, he offered me a ride home. He was surprised to hear my story. He said he had called the railroad police on hobos before and now he was aiding and abetting.

So, is it tougher to ride trains now? It does not seem so. But I have been meditating several hours a day for over twenty years, so it could simply be that my karma has gotten better than railroad security. We make our own luck, with a lot of help from our amazing friend — Grace.

A frustrated Italian immigrant, working on the highway in Utah's Spanish Fork Canyon in the 1930s, reportedly said, "I no lika thesa Uniteda States. I wanna go back to Helper." I wanted to go back, too. In September 2005, coffeehouse conversation with my friends, Susan and Chris in Salt Lake City, had turned to Helper, Utah. Susan said it was fast becoming an artist colony and had a rescue mission. I knew it as a railroad town and decided to explore these developments further. It turned out that buses didn't stop there anymore and I couldn't get Amtrak tickets, so it was either hop freights or skip Helper and jump to Denver. My huge, fancy Arcteryx backpack was not ideal for hoboing.

The former Denver and Rio Grande (now Union Pacific) yards in Salt Lake City are just west of Interstate 15 between 2100 South and 3300 South. In the past, I had always entered the yard from the north end, but, in preparation for the 2002 Winter Olympics, the city had reworked the freeway system and created a complicated spaghetti junction in that area. While meditating, it hit me: why not avoid all that confusion and enter the yard from the south end? I caught another Olympic addition, light rail, to the 3300 South exit. I walked west a short distance to a railroad overpass, climbed the embankment, and was in the yard by 8:45 pm. If life gets too complicated and your mind is a spaghetti junction, go into the silence. Your "still small voice" will give you the best alternative.

I walked north up the tracks and went straight to a yardman, who told me where my train to Helper would be built. He also said it would be early morning before the train would depart. Finally, he warned me to avoid the Jeeps that the railroad cops drove. The yard was brilliantly lit and hiding places were scarce. Fortunately, a crane sat at the end of the yard, so I climbed up into the relative safety of its cab. High off the ground with the sun flaps down, I could see out but others couldn't see in.

Around midnight, I got stiff and cold, so I walked around the yard, keeping the lowest of profiles. Finally, two engines attached themselves to my string of cars. But long-run trains usually have three *units*. The last time I left this yard on a train with only two engines, I ended up on a work train headed in the wrong direction. I was suspicious, but climbed inside the back *unit* to warm up and observe the action in the yard. It was too cozy and I fell asleep.

A yardman woke me and told me I'd better get off. I asked where the train was going and he said Grand Junction, Colorado. When I told him I would find another car, he said, "Aw, just hide out in the bathroom and stay there until the train starts to move." I obeyed and we departed at 6:15 am. The train stopped to pick up a lumber car near the pass at Soldier Summit at 8:30 am. Another railroad worker came in my *unit*, but thankfully ignored me.

At 11:15 a.m. the train pulled into Helper. I climbed off and took a minute to get my bearings.

My first stop was the Helper Antique Mall where I found Susan's friend, Kelly. We chatted and I then went to the "Back to the 50s Diner" for lunch. I wandered Main Street and then headed to the Golden Rule Mission in the old Avalon Hotel building. I was self-conscious because I didn't think I looked "down and out" enough. But the man behind the desk said he had seen me walking the streets, and was wondering when I would finally check in. I filled out paperwork and went upstairs to clean up. A sign in the bathroom said, "Do not flush the toilet when someone is showering." Wise words to live by.

I explored Helper, did some research at the library and the Western Mining and Railroad Museum, meditated in the park and went back to the mission for dinner. My meal consisted of rice soup, donated by a local café, and a large helping of body-fluid-reddening beets. Later, the mission showed an intriguing Wim Winders film called *Million Dollar Hotel* (about a bunch of crazy people living in a run-down hotel) in their lobby. Most of the crazy people in the run-down Helper hotel disliked it and requested a John Wayne movie. Just before the mission's ten o'clock curfew, I decided to check out and catch a freight train to Colorado. I sent the mission a donation after I returned home.

The best spot to wait for a train at night in Helper is behind the garages of St. Anthony's Catholic Church, which provide concealing shadows. I meditated for an hour and at 1:00 a.m. a train pulled in from the north. I had to move fast if I wanted to ride in an engine. When the train slowed sufficiently, I climbed up a ladder of a grain car, walked across the catwalk, went down the ladder on the other side and jumped off. With the train as my screen, I *two-tied it* (taking two ties per stride) for the front of the train, which had stopped by the yard office. If the crew change took place quickly, I would have to get on another car, so I checked them out as I moved forward, looking for good places to ride. Luckily, the crew change took longer than usual, so I made it to the second *unit*. Once again, there were only two engines. The entrance to my engine was on the west side, which was brightly illuminated, and also next to the yard office where I could easily be seen. I waited in the shadows on the engine's east side runway until the train finally pulled out, so I could move into the cab under the cover of darkness.

Since the last time I rode this line in 1983, there had been a great increase in lighting — as was true in most yards. There are two schools of thought regarding train yard security: 1) provide more railroad police, which is expensive; and 2) provide greater candlepower, which is cheaper. There are also different ways to make human progress. People can find self-help gurus or psychotherapists. They can be beneficial, but are often pricey. Another is by meditation. It is Divine Psychotherapy. You become illuminated. The light comes from within.

Trinidad, Colorado is the sex-change capitol of the world, although one would never suspect it. It was a stopping place on the Mountain Branch of the old Santa Fe Trail. Agriculture was its original economic mainstay, then coal mining. It became a railroad center in the 1870s. Wyatt Earp, Bat Masterson, Billy the Kid and Kit Carson all had connections to Trinidad. Built during boom times, the following busts left the town too poor to afford to tear down buildings and erect new ones. The town is the richer for it. It is also a railroad crew change point. It should have been an easy place to *catch out.*

I rode into town on a bus in September 2005 on my way home from Alaska. I wasn't having any gender issues, but I did want to explore the town because I plan to have a murder take place in Trinidad in the screenplay of this book. I also wanted to ride a freight train from Trinidad to Amarillo, Texas through the mesa-laden northeast corner of New Mexico, where I had never hopped.

My first stop in Trinidad was the Colorado Welcome Center. I spoke with a well-informed local named Joe. He filled me in on many subjects, including more than I wanted to know about sex-change operations. He said that the animated television series *South Park* even did a typically tasteless episode about the procedure. Dr. Stanley Biber performed his first sex-change operation in 1969 and eventually averaged 165 per year. He was forced into retirement at age eighty-one because he could no longer get malpractice insurance. His practice was taken over by an eminently qualified doctor, Marci Bowers, who was once a man herself. The surgery alone costs $14,000, but the procedure is simple. Bowers once told a patient, "It's like rearranging the deck chairs." Biber died the same day that Felicity Huffman won a Golden Globe Award for her poignant portrayal of a pre-operative male-to-female transsexual in the film *Transamerica.*

The staff at the Welcome Center let me stash my gigantic backpack in their break room. Armed with pamphlets, I did Trinidad's historic walking tour. The scenery in all directions is superb, with the Sangre de Cristo Mountains to the west; the Spanish Peaks to the north; Fisher's Peak to the south; and Simpson's Rest to the northwest. The Purgatoire River runs through it. The historic district is one of the most intact I have witnessed. Adobe, sandstone and brick produce eclectic architectural styles. I went to the library and did research. Two friendly drunks in a city park offered me beer and food.

I retrieved my enormous pack about an hour before nightfall, and began a slow shuffle to the train yards at the northern edge of town. I saw a fox, which to some symbolizes camouflage — something I would need to avoid detection. Near a Halliburton yard where Freedom Road crosses the railroad tracks, I followed the steel rails into the descending darkness until I came to a well-lit area where the tracks split four ways. This was clearly a crew change point. I crawled through a hole in the fence, found a dark cove and waited.

Trains hauling coal from Wyoming to Texas were supposed to run through Trinidad and return empty. Trains heading north stopped with great regularity. Most of the trains had two engines in front and one in back. I occasionally climbed into one of the back engines to warm up. One engine just came from the factory and emitted that "new car" smell. Once I fell asleep. When the train finally left, I had to exit quickly because, pulling empties, it accelerated rapidly. But no trains were heading south.

I eventually decided to walk up a gravel road toward the yard office, where the front end of the trains stopped. I needed information, but there were no yardmen working there to query. The northbound trains continued to come all night, change crews and leave. Van drivers whisked the rail employees away to their nights lodging. Still nothing went south.

At about 7:00 a.m., yard office workers started to arrive for their workday. I stepped out of my dark sanctuary and asked one of them why there were no trains heading south. He told me that the railroad had just started to run loaded coal trains through La Junta, Colorado and Boise City, Oklahoma on their way to Amarillo, Texas. Only the empties ran back through Trinidad. The truth shall set you free, but first it will make you miserable.

I had been up all night, and I was too tired to trek the several miles back to town. Instead, I walked to the nearby freeway and stuck out my thumb. A woman, who worked with developmentally disabled people, picked me up on the way to her agency. Since I had worked at a "sheltered workshop" in Glenwood Springs, Colorado, we had a nice conversation. She gave me a ride to a gas station that doubled as the bus stop. I bought a ticket for Oklahoma City and called my honeylamb with the arrival time. The bus finally came at midnight. I had a four-hour layover in Raton, New Mexico. I crawled in my sleeping bag and slept in a darling little McDonald's parking lot where the buses stopped. It wasn't pretty, but I was finally on the last leg of my journey from Alaska to "Okrahoma."

The great Harmonic Convergence ushered in a new era on August 17, 1987. Shirley MacLaine said so. At the time, I was stuck in a traffic jam on an entrance ramp to the Hollywood Freeway in Los Angeles, California. "This must be the Harmonic Convergence," I cynically quipped to my fellow monks. Trinidad had its own harmonic convergence. At the same time the railroad stopped running loaded coal trains through town, the Trinidad hospital stopped doing female to male sex changes. But empty trains still run through town, and men are still changed into women.

The moral of this story is: Don't look for a moral in every story.

I made a pilgrimage to Rock Island Arsenal in the Quad Cities area of Illinois and Iowa in October 2005. Rock Island is the largest island on the Mississippi River. The United States acquired title to it in 1804, and set it aside as a military reservation in 1809. In addition, the first railroad bridge over the Mississippi used it as a stepping-stone in 1856. That's what piqued my interest.

My friend Scott drove me to Rock Island, and we walked across Government Bridge, which replaced the original structure — in a better location — in 1872. Scott didn't have a picture ID, so the Arsenal guards at the south gate surrounded us. While they ran computer checks on us, the bridge's unique swing span rotated open to let a ship pass through. Unfortunately, security wouldn't let Scott in the Arsenal area, so we returned to his house. I got my car and drove alone through the north gate for a thorough exploration of the island.

George Davenport became the first white settler in the region in 1816 when he moved to Rock Island. He was a non-military provisioner during the construction of Fort Armstrong on the island. Davenport soon created his own empire with nine trading posts and a fleet of boats to serve them. He was a mediator between Indians and the Government during the Black Hawk War of 1832. In 1833, he built his "federal style" dream house on the island. In June 1845, he and a group of investors met in his home to plan a railroad into the area. Davenport did not live to see his dream come to fruition. Robbers murdered him in his home a month later. However, Davenport's plans eventually led to the construction of America's first railroad bridge across a navigable river.

One of the reasons I was intrigued with the bridge had to do with Abraham Lincoln. Before he emancipated the slaves, he liberated hobos to be able to travel across the country freely. He did this by helping railroads break the steamboat owners' monopoly on shipping. Two other people who would go on to have major roles in the Civil War also played a part in this drama — Jefferson Davis and Robert E. Lee.

Lincoln believed that railroads were crucial to help America transform from a subsistence economy to a market economy. In 1853, he did his first railroad work as a lawyer for the Illinois Central Railroad that Casey Jones bravely engineered. He won two important cases for them, but had to sue them to get paid. However it was Lincoln's efforts in *Hurd v. Rock Island Railroad Company* that made him famous and broke the steamboaters' stranglehold on shipping.

Steamboat interests rightly feared that railroads would eventually make shipping on the rivers less lucrative if navigable rivers were bridged and the railroads built a transcontinental system. They petitioned Jefferson Davis, the Secretary of War at the time, to disallow the use of the federally owned island for the bridge's construction. Even amidst their protests, approval for the structure came through in 1854.

Fifteen days after the Rock Island Bridge became operational in 1856, a side-wheel steamboat, the *Effie Afton*, crashed into one of its piers, caught fire and burned. The collision knocked a portion of the bridge into the river. The rest of the bridge caught fire and was destroyed. Steamboat captains blew their whistles in delight. Investigators suspected, but never proved, that the crash was not an accident. Hurd, the owner of the *Effie Afton*, sued in Illinois to recover the cost of his boat and to prevent the rebuilding of that bridge, or any future bridges on the Mississippi, which he claimed were a hazard to navigation. The Rock Island Railroad hired Abraham Lincoln to try the case.

Lincoln did his homework. He examined the bridge, river currents, steamboat operations and the crash itself. He took his own meticulous measurements. He also studied a survey of the rapids near the bridge completed in 1837 by "the" Lt. Robert E. Lee of the U.S. Army Corps of Engineers. At the informal trial, Lincoln whittled on a stick and then carved up the litigant's case. The trial ended in a hung jury, which was a victory for Lincoln and the Rock Island Railroad. The Supreme Court eventually decided a subsequent suit in the railroad's favor in 1862.

This pivotal case solidified Lincoln's reputation as a great trial lawyer. The resultant fame and the money he made on the case put him in a position to run for President three years later. After he became President in 1860, Lincoln formally inaugurated construction of the first transcontinental railroad.

Entrenched interests try to stop progress. That includes egos. They sabotage spiritual efforts. The Hindus have a saying, "When the ego goes, God comes." Egos do not go easily. We will need an Emancipator. Our egos will tell us otherwise.

In August 2006, I caught a BNSF coal train in Amarillo, Texas and rode it through a corner of New Mexico into Trinidad, Colorado. This left South Dakota as the only state west of the Mississippi where I had not yet hopped. This caper began when I drove to Amarillo and left my car in BNSF's North Yard parking lot just after dark. I explored the yard and found a good place to hide. Five hours later, an empty coal train pulled up. I had planned to get in one of the head-end *units,* but this train was an anomaly — it only had one engine in front. I hustled toward the *helper* engine, which I hoped was on the back end of the train. Coal trains can be over one hundred cars long. Fortunately, I got to the rear of the train before it *highballed.* As a precaution, I initially hid in the bathroom.

An hour later, the front door to the engine compartment opened and a black man entered. I wondered where he came from, as he could not possibly have jumped on the train traveling at fifty-miles per hour. Drew had hopped on in Amarillo, too, but, upon entering the nose compartment of the cab, had spied me through the inner door's window. He thought I might be a railroad employee, so he stayed put. Finally, when it got too cold and noisy, he took a chance and came into the engine compartment. Drew wanted to get off in Dalhart, Texas in order to catch a Union Pacific train to Tucumcari, New Mexico and eventually California, where he lived. The cordial man was able to hop off when the train slowed to a speed of twenty miles per hour. He had made his little leap of faith unscathed and he raised his arms in triumph, let out a whoop and gave me a big wave.

At dawn, the train reached the enchanting mesa country of New Mexico. By sunrise, we had crossed the border into Colorado. We arrived in that now extremely familiar yard in Trinidad at 8:45 a.m. I disembarked and took the informative, free trolley tour of town. On the return trip from the hospital and its famous 3D ceramic mural, I checked into the Trails End Motel – a classic fifties-era establishment run by bikers. After a shower and meditation, I went to the Rino Restaurant in the old Christian Church building for lunch. I took a tour of the Baca and Bloom House museums, and had dinner at an old railroad depot that now housed a restaurant. I explored other landmarks, and then dropped into the classic Monte Cristo Bar. One customer looked like he was "going through the change." Prior to the actual operation, sex-change candidates get their Adam's apples shaved off, take hormones, get breast implants and dress as women for at least a year. Before making such major life-changing decisions, it's best to test-drive them as much as possible. Candidates for most monastic orders are required to live the lifestyle for long periods before officially joining, so the monastery knows what they are getting and the candidates know what to expect. Celibacy is not hereditary.

The next morning, I walked to the Hot Spot Café in the historic Savoy Hotel for breakfast. The tattooed owners of my motel came in later, and an intriguing old man occupied the booth next to mine. I saw him later on a street bench and stopped to chat. I have a soft spot for such characters, as I will no doubt be one some day.

As I walked to the Amtrak station, I noticed that the Catholic Church's steeple was a fraction taller than the old, defunct brewery's tower — as if they had been competing for attention and influence. Unbelievably, my passenger train was on time, but my prepaid reservation was not on the conductor's list. I had to pay a second fare and was not pleased. The short train ride to Raton, New Mexico went by Dick Wootton's ranch along the old toll road he built in 1865, and then through a tunnel at Raton Pass. At nearly four-percent, Raton Pass is the steepest main line grade still in use.

We arrived in Raton at 11:00 a.m. I did a historic walking tour, then hoofed to the edge of town and began an all-day ordeal. First I hitched for four hours in the broiling sun, then I spent four more hours in a deluge in Capulin, New Mexico. I finally checked into a motel in Des Moines, New Mexico for the night and tried to dry out. The next morning, it only took thirty minutes to get a ride all the way to Amarillo from Paul, who was going to his brother's Golden Anniversary celebration in Alabama. I retrieved my car, and picked up a drunk, Navaho bull rider, who was hitchhiking to Arkansas.

Prior to starting this adventure, I checked Map Quest on the Internet. It indicated that trains leaving Amarillo in a westerly direction would either veer southwest or northwest shortly after leaving the yard. The yard had a northern and a southern set of tracks on the west end of the yard about a block apart, so naturally I assumed that I could catch the northwest bound train on the northernmost track. But an empty coal train — that should have been heading north to the Wyoming coalfields — left on the southern tracks, so I did not try to hop it. Later, as I walked west along the tracks, avoiding the waiting *bulls,* I came to a place where the southernmost tracks crossed under the northern tracks and headed northwest. That earlier coal train was going in my direction after all, but had I caught it, I would have gone through the most spectacular part of the trip before dawn.

My monastic life took a similar turn. My initial intention was to remain a monk for life. But about five years in, I hit a wall. Like a runner, I planned to keep going until I broke through it. But two of the organization's spiritual giants, who knew me better than I knew myself, concluded that I had gotten all I was going to get out of monastic life and said I would make more progress outside of the order. I knew immediately that they were right. I was totally impressed by their integrity, because I was a key production planner in the organization's print shop. Still, they did what was best for me and, ultimately, best for the organization. My monastic track went south, but had I not taken that track when I did I would have gone through life in the dark.

⊫ CHAPTER 37: THEFT OF SERVICE ⟪⟫

I had a chance meeting with a performer from the Obviously Unrehearsed Improvisational Comedy group in Norman, Oklahoma in 2005. Curt had read Duffy Littlejohn's book *Riding Freight Trains in America* and wanted to hop. We exchanged addresses, but lost touch. A year later, we met again. It seemed fortuitous. He was the same age as I was when I first hopped and reminded me of myself. Was it time to pass the mantle like Elijah did to Elisha and go to heaven in a flash of fire?

In early November, I proposed a bunny hop with training wheels — a passenger train to Gainesville, Texas and a freight train back. Oddly enough, at exactly the same time we were plotting our caper, a couple of crackers were stealing copper wire along two miles of the track we were about to traverse. The wire merely carried communications information vital to the safe operation of the railway. Fortunately, they were apprehended by a railroad cop I met once for coffee years earlier.

We dropped my car off near the Oklahoma City Burlington Northern Santa Fe (BNSF) rail yard the day before and met at the Norman depot on a Sunday to catch the Amtrak. The redneck conductor rudely informed us that we couldn't ride in the front car because the ride was too rough and the train whistle would drive us nuts. Little did he know that our next ride would be on a *rattler*. He later did the Texas tongue laugh — sticking his tongue down to the bottom of his chin while chortling. I told Curt that he would have been exactly like him if his parents had not moved from Red Oak to Tulsa, Oklahoma. We quietly, but sardonically, mimicked a woman across from us who encouraged her grandson to write a story about the train ride, but then proceeded to dictate the tale to him and spell the harder words.

When we got to Gainesville, we explored the museum in the restored Santa Fe depot. It gave us an encapsulated history of the town. French trappers, Spanish gold seekers and Louisiana Purchase explorers moved through the area that was part of the Native American's Wichita Confederation. Gainesville voted to stay in the Union during the Civil War but Texas didn't. Because of that vote, Confederate sympathizers staged the "Great Hanging" and lynched forty Gainesville residents in 1862. Gainesville enjoyed a cattle boom after the Civil War because it was situated at the fork of the Chisholm and Shawnee Trails. The famous Butterfield Stage went through town as well. Gainesville is also unique in that it had a Community Circus, from 1930 to 1964, that featured citizen performers.

The Dennison and Pacific Railway (D&P) completed track from Dennison, Texas and in 1879 the first locomotive entered town. In 1880, the Missouri, Kansas & Texas Railroad (the MKT, aka the Katy) acquired the D&P. Galveston businessmen started Gulf, Colorado and Santa Fe Railroad in 1873 and it reached Gainesville in 1887. In 1886, the town was linked to the Atchison, Topeka, and the Santa Fe Railway (ATSF). In 1902, the ATSF depot was built, which included a famous Harvey House lunch counter. In its heyday during World War II, Gainesville was eighth in the nation in passenger ticket sales, but by 1979 passenger train service was terminated and the depot abandoned. The structure was deeded to the city in 1981 and renovated. Amtrak began service to Gainesville in 1999.

Curt and I walked to the 306 Blues and BBQ restaurant for lunch. Their motto was "to drink is human, to lounge is divine." The liquor stores were closed so, after eating, we headed for the tracks without our "flight insurance."

The first two freight trains blew through the yard without stopping for a crew change. I sensed that something was wrong, so we immediately headed to the yard office for information. A railroad employee, who said he harbored an urge to hop himself, told us that the trains no longer changed crews in Gainesville. We now had three options: 1) hitchhike to Oklahoma; 2) go back to the cafe and divinely lounge until the passenger train returned to Norman; or 3) wait near the yard in case a freight stopped to add or drop cars. I left the decision up to Curt. He chose to wait for the unlikely stop of a freight train. If one didn't stop by 6:00 p.m., we decided that we would ride *on the cushions* back to Norman. We found an abandoned *hobo jungle*, did an informal archeological dig and waited.

Fifteen minutes before our "give up" time, we heard a northbound train. It stopped on the south side of the yard office — which was unusual — and then started up again. We raced toward it to board before it got going too fast. It veered off the main line, so we crossed several lines of cars and hid until the engines emerged. After the lead engine passed us, we leapt on to the third *unit* and hustled into the cab. Our miracle stop had happened and Curt joined the Benevolent and Defective Order of Trundlers.

God helps those who help themselves. The cliché is correct. As Curt suggested, by choosing to wait by the tracks instead of in the comfortable cafe, we put ourselves in position for success. Something similar happened to me when I was hired as the town manager of Brian Head, Utah. My first task was to finish an already late grant application. Our chances of getting it were nil, but it would not have looked good to beg-off so early in my employment. As expected, we did not get any money, but the following year another round of grants was announced. This time only those who applied the previous year could get money. Happily, our frozen water lines got replaced.

The grants called for matching funds. We put in twenty-five percent; the federal government put up the remaining seventy-five percent. This is like Grace. God overmatches every effort we make to do good — whether we believe it or not.

Our train out of Gainesville went about a hundred yards and stopped. Two rail employees got off the lead engine and walked toward the rear of the train. The train then began to move forward, but it stopped a short distance later and went into reverse. This usually means that some cars are getting *set off*, and the chances of someone coming into our *unit* skyrocketed. A singing brakeman did just that and was startled by our presence. He was friendly enough and provided useful information. He went to the fourth *unit* and told his partner that they had riders. His buddy came over with a six-pack of bottled drinking water for us. He respectfully asked us if we were "professional train riders." Without hesitation, I said, "Yes." I nearly added, "I've been riding since 1973; Curt since 6:04 p.m." He said, "You don't get us in trouble; we won't get you in trouble." Then he turned on the cab's radio so we could listen to the dispatcher's instructions to the various trains.

Cars were *set off* and others picked up. Finally, our low priority train eased out. The rough ride and train horn did not drive us nuts as predicted by the Texas tongue laugher. We mimicked the dictating grandmother. "The train was dirty, D-I-R-T-Y, and loud, L-O-U-D, and when they caught us riding it, they put us in jail, J-A-I-L." We were treated to a fierce lightning show to the east, while lounging on the back platform. Curt puffed on a cigar.

We got to Noble, Oklahoma, only a few miles from our homes in Norman, by 11:00 p.m., but our train stopped for an eternity on the main line. Against my instructions, Curt had secretly brought his cell phone. He powered it up and I called my wife with a progress report. Soon after, the train sprinted to Norman and, as I had predicted, went *into the hole* on the north side of town next to a southbound train. The southbound left and I assumed that we would do so soon afterwards. Instead, we sat there blocking a major intersection for thirty minutes until a higher priority freight train passed us.

Finally, the train departed, but when we got to the BNSF yard the speedometer read a dangerous forty-miles per hour. As we flew past my getaway car, Curt comically asked, "Do you have any friends in Kansas?" When the speedometer registered twenty-miles per hour, about five miles later, I told Curt to get ready. We emerged from the cab and got on the stairways of the second and third engines. Curt tested the speed as I had taught him by dropping his legs to the ground but hanging on to the railings so he could pull himself up — if necessary. The train was still going too fast. We came to a grade crossing at Grand Avenue and I got off *on the fly*. Curt came right after me. We were stoked. We trudged back to my car and gleefully got to Norman at 3:00 a.m.

Three days later, I e-mailed Curt and warned him about a side effect of freight train hopping, a Cheshire cat grin that stays on the face for five to seven days. Guilty as charged was his reply. I suggested a naming ceremony whereby I would bestow a *hobo handle* on him. He loved the idea. The sacred event took place at Curt's home with a few of his friends in attendance. The mantle itself was a sleeping bag, since Curt learned that a hobo should always carry a bedroll. The crown was a dunce cap made out of a gallon plastic jug — like the one Curt foolishly carried in one hand while trying to scramble across rail cars. I tied dental floss around his finger to remind him to never practice oral hygiene in a *hobo jungle* again. I presented him with a can of "Hobo Soup" and a "Do Not Hump" sign. I sprinkled him three times with German wheat beer while incanting, "In the name of the Locomotive, and the Boxcar, and the Vanishing Caboose," I tapped him on the shoulders with the flare that the he took from our engine and said, "I dub thee 'Flare.'" In honor of the time when an automated voice in our engine informed us that the train had "no defects," and I had hollered back, "What about the two guys in the third *unit*?" — I dubbed us "The Defects." I told him about the twelve-step group for freight riding addicts that meets at the International House of Pancakes. They start each testimony by saying, "My name is _____ and I hop." After the ceremony, we sat around a fire in Curt's backyard. *Hobo jungle*-like, but with people I trusted, I did a number of appropriately irresponsible things.

I reread the biblical story of Elijah's mantle falling on Elisha and the circumstantial parallels were eerie. I told Curt he could hide in the engine's bathroom in Gainesville so that if I got caught he would not be detected. In Noble and again at the Rock Creek crossing in Norman, I suggested that he get off the train without me and walk home. His attitude was, "We start the adventure together; we finish the adventure together." Elisha refused to leave Elijah in Gilgal, Bethel, and Jericho, saying, "As the Lord lives, and as you yourself live, I will not leave you." Elisha received a double share of Elijah's spirit. Because so many things went wrong on our trip, Curt was forced to absorb a double share of unexpected lessons — like getting off a moving train at a relatively high rate of speed, which is not recommended for a first hop. Now, Elijah-like, I've been sucked up into the whirlwind of book publishing and promotion. But I doubt that it will take me to heaven.

I do not believe that it matters what we believe. God works with our honest mistakes. What matters is how we act on our beliefs. Before we got off that moving freight train, I also safety-tested by putting just my lead foot down. If contact with the ground forces your foot up so hard that it kicks you in the butt, the train is going too fast. Similarly, we should first test our beliefs with small actions. If our exploration results in a kick in the butt, we need to reevaluate before we leap to our demise. (Then former followers of a certain charlatan in Oregon would have no need to say, "Why can't we just let Bhagwans be Bhagwans?") If our little tests are successful, we can gradually ramp up the experiment and live life *on the fly.*

In April 1909 — for the first time in recorded history — Alaska's Miles Glacier began to surge in winter. The timing couldn't have been worse. E. C. Hawkins, the chief engineer of the fabled Copper River and Northwest Railroad (CR&NW), was desperately trying to place the steel on the most critical span of the Million Dollar Bridge before the river ice broke up in the spring.

Most people who studied rail routes to the fabulously wealthy Kennecott Copper Mine had determined that the Copper River could not be bridged between the Child and Miles Glaciers and recommended routes out of Valdez, Alaska. Hawkins said it could be spanned. So did Mike Heney, who was Hawkins' general contractor on the equally amazing White Pass and Yukon Route railroad. Daniel Guggenheim of the notorious Alaska Syndicate bet his money on the advice of these two railroad veterans. His previous gamble, building a port on the east side of the Copper River Delta in unprotected Katalla, was a failure. Violent storms out of the Gulf of Alaska in the fall of 1907 destroyed millions of dollars worth of work there. Now they were building out of the protected harbor of Cordova on the west side of the Delta, but failure was again tapping them on their shoulders.

The four bridge spans were thirty-feet above the river and had to be supported below by wooden falsework until the steel could be bolted into place. The Miles Glacier's relentless advance was now up against the scaffolding of the third span. Hawkins had thirty Scandinavians constantly chiseling the river of ice away from the woodwork, with wind chill factors approaching minus-sixty degrees. Uff da! The workmen won the battle. Hours after the last bolt was secured, the glacier destroyed the falsework. The bridge itself, the world's first example of major "arctic engineering," was not damaged. In fact, it is now considered one of the greatest engineering marvels of all time. It stood strong until the largest earthquake in North American history occurred on Good Friday in 1964. Even then, when other, newer bridges were twisted into oblivion, only one pier of the Million Dollar Bridge was seriously damaged, and only one end of the fourth span fell into the silt-laden river.

In March 1911, the copper spike was driven signaling the completion of the CR&NW rail line, nicknamed "Can't Run and Never Will." The first shipment of copper ore arrived in Cordova for transport to the smelter in April of that year. The train ran until November 1938. Depletion of the ore body and falling copper prices during the Great Depression created the double whammy that ended the railroad's spectacular run. In 1941, the Alaska Syndicate conveyed the right-of-way to the Federal Government for use as a public highway. In 2005, the fourth span was raised at a cost of ten million dollars. It is now jokingly referred to as the "Eleven Million

Dollar Bridge." The bridge to somewhere now leads nowhere. The mostly dirt road ends at mile 49 out of Cordova, just past the bridge. It begins again near Chitina at mile 128 and runs a tire-eating sixty-miles to the town of McCarthy. Many in Cordova do not want the road completed because of the potential for opening the tourist floodgates.

I had done a cursory exploration of both ends of the rail line in 2003. But in May 2009, I drove up on the Alaska Highway and took my vehicle for an extended visit of the McCarthy and Kennecott areas. In June, four Denali friends and I planned a Cordova caper. J.J., Amanda, Keith, Serena and I drove to Valdez and ferried to Cordova with a car. A deluge determined that we spend our first night in the classic 1908 Alaskan Hotel. In the hotel bar, we heard a man named Dave playing a twelve-string guitar. It was strung for a right-handed person, but this lefty had learned to play it upside down. J. J. is also an accomplished musician. The two of them passed the instrument back and forth and "sang up every song this driver knew." Locals drifted in and out and provided chain-smoking harmonies. I rarely frequent taverns, but this night was musically marvelous.

The next day greeted us with partly cloudy skies, so we drove through the Copper River Delta — the largest wetland on the Pacific Coast of North America — and across the resurrected Million Dollar Bridge. The Miles Glacier had shyly retreated five miles, but the Child Glacier still loomed majestically a hundred and fifty yards across the river and calved into its chilly waters. We listened to the rifle-fire cracking of the glacier, ate ice worms and fed mosquitoes until late into the night.

The CR&NW was the last project for E. C. Hawkins and Mike Heney (called "H and H" by their adoring workers). In August 1909, Heney was on the steamboat *Ohio* heading to Alaska with railroad supplies. The ship hit an uncharted rock and sank. Heney was pitched into the frigid sea. He survived the ordeal, but his health was severely compromised. He died of pulmonary tuberculosis in October 1910. Hawkins wept, but he and his men were determined to finish the job for "The Boss." Hawkins retired in October 1911, after completing the task. One year after the first shipment of copper ore reached Cordova, Hawkins had surgery for kidney stones in New York. He died the next day. The team of "H and H" was no more. I still wonder if they went to "H or H."

The Million Dollar Bridge was the lynch pin for the railroad that shipped 200 million dollars worth of copper ore and raked in a hundred million dollars in profits for the Alaska Syndicate. Likewise, life force is the link between mind and matter. Proper life force control (*pranayama*), utilizing will power and concentration, will determine whether we build bridges to nowhere or somewhere.

I only rode in one caboose (although I sometimes bummed toilet paper from those crew members in the back). It was early in my train-hopping career. I was headed for the mountains in Colorado and was trying to hop a Burlington Northern train out of Chicago, Illinois. As my train was pulling out, I spied an extra caboose in the middle of the train, deadheading west, so I climbed on board. With padded benches long enough to sleep on and a cupola observation deck, it was better than riding in an engine. A yardman had told me earlier that they were going to split the train in Lincoln, Nebraska — with half continuing to Denver, Colorado and the remainder heading to Wyoming.

When we pulled into Lincoln to change crews and fuel up, I asked a crabby yardman if the caboose half was going to Denver. He grunted an affirmation. Normally, yardmen are good people who give reliable information, and I wanted to believe him and stay in that cozy caboose. But I didn't follow my own rule — always get at least three confirmations about your train's destination. Meanwhile, the other rail cars had left the yard and I fell asleep in the cupola of the stationary caboose. Another yardman came through the caboose later that night and gave me the bad news: I was on the Wyoming half of the train. I had to wait nearly twelve hours for the next Colorado-bound freight.

The caboose evolved to provide the rear train crew — the conductor, brakeman, and flagman — with shelter. From there they could switch the tracks and protect the rear of the train when stopped. They could also inspect the train for shifting loads, broken equipment and overheated bearings in *hotboxes*. The conductor, who is the crewmember in charge of a train, managed its operation from the caboose. The caboose often provided bunks, stoves, and toilets, and was frequently decorated. The caboose's location at the end of the train, however, made it a dangerous place to work. *Slack action* (which occurs when a train suddenly starts, stops, or changes speed) could severely jolt a caboose. A toppled lantern could start a fire, and derailments and rear-end collisions were often fatal.

The origin of the caboose has been traced to Nat Williams, a conductor on the Auburn & Syracuse Railroad during the 1830s, who began directing freight train operations from the last car. Most cabooses had a cupola on top where the crew inspected the train. T. B. Watson, a conductor on the Chicago and North Western Railway, conceived the idea for the cupola. In 1863, his regular caboose was reassigned and he was given an empty boxcar to use. The boxcar's roof had a hole in it and Watson sat on boxes with his head sticking through the opening to inspect the train. He later suggested that a similar structure be added to the top of future cabooses. Freight cars in the late 1920s were often taller than most cupolas, so the bay window caboose was invented. The crew sat in a section of wall that projected from the side of the caboose.

The first usage in print of "caboose" was in 1861. Railroad historian David L. Joslyn believes the word derived from the Low German *kabhuse*, a wooden cabin on a ship's deck, or the Middle Dutch word *kabuis*, the compartment on a ship's deck where the cooking was done. The first cabooses, like the nautical versions, were either wooden huts built on flatcars or modified boxcars. Another theory claims the word originated in Texas (doesn't everything?) from the Spanish word *calabozo*, meaning jailhouse.

Sometimes called a *way car* in the eastern portion of the United States, the caboose was traditionally painted bright red. After a while, these American icons were painted the same color as their locomotives. By the mid-1920s, there were an estimated 34,000 cabooses in operation, but today only a few hundred cabooses remain active on smaller *shortline* railroads. Many cabooses are now in railway museums or used as visitor centers.

Until the 1980s, laws required that all freight trains have a caboose, but electronic monitors rendered them obsolete. Spaced roughly a dozen miles apart, the monitors detect dragging equipment, out-of-round wheels, hot journal bearings and shifting loads. An electronic box named FRED, an acronym for *flashing rear-end device*, is also attached to the back of the train. It functions as a warning beacon, detects the train's air brake pressure and lets the engineer know when the slack is out of the couplings so additional power can be applied. This information is reported to the crew in the locomotives by an obnoxious, synthesized voice. The conductor now rides in the front of the train.

As technology made the caboose obsolete, intuition renders the intellect less important. (St. Thomas Aquinas could not finish his philosophic masterpiece, *Summa Theologica*, after a mystic experience, calling it "so much straw.") Intuition is the ability to tap the soul's innate all-knowingness. If we are not vigilant, however, the ego can co-opt intuition. The "still small voice" of God is in competition with the "big loud mouth" of ego. Wishful thinking, emotionalism, habit and other imposters masquerade as intuition. Keeping the intuitional channel open requires regular daily deep meditation, regular introspection, and, ironically, the use of the intellect. Facts still have to be gathered and analyzed linearly before they are turned over to the intuition for lateral thinking. The intellect should be the servant, not the master, of the inner guidance of intuition, which can instantaneously give us what the intellect can only approximate. For all of your getting, get intuition.

If you are now enraptured by my book, tempted to join my cult, and call me Yahwayne, let me emphasize that I am a lesser teacher. What I have given you are appetizers. You need to go elsewhere for the full meal.

When the student is ready, the teacher appears, but when the student is ready to move beyond mere spiritual dabblings and get serious about meditation, an Emancipator with a mystic path appears (Hindus call this person the guru). Again, it takes a great deal of discrimination to find a true mystic teaching. There are many pitfalls, including the one that says, "I can cobble together my own meditation methods." I don't believe we can hodge-podge our way to God with some Frankenstein faith. Mixing meditation methods is like mixing pharmaceuticals — some cancel each other out; some result in dangerous combinations. Nor do I believe that we can keep jumping from mystic path to mystic path. A relationship with God is very much like human relationships. There is a "dating phase," where we explore various options, but it can't last forever. To progress, we have to make a serious commitment or risk becoming what I call a "spiritualizer" — the equivalent of a womanizer.

While there are many mystic paths out there in all the great religions, there are only two that I know inside out and can heartily recommend. (Neither condones freight train hopping). First and foremost are the precepts of Paramahansa Yogananda, best found initially in his spiritual classic *Autobiography of a Yogi*. Yogananda's revelatory interpretations of Christian scripture, elaborated in *The Second Coming of Christ: The Resurrection of the Christ Within You*, were the first to ring true for me. Yogananda created Self-Realization Fellowship (SRF) to be the sole disseminator of his writings, so make sure you get his material from that organization (www.yogananda-srf.org).

If you are uncomfortable going outside of mainstream Christianity, then I endorse the work of Thomas Keating and his organization, Contemplative Outreach (www.contemplativeoutreach.org). I suggest starting with his book *Open Mind, Open Heart*. If Catholics had not ignored the contemplative dimension of the Gospel for centuries, there may not have been a need for the Reformation. Keating is bringing long-lost contemplative methods back from obscurity and making them relevant for today. Of all the Christian faiths I have examined, only the Catholics seem to have the tools that lead to spiritual ecstasy. Fortunately, they are sharing the Christian contemplative tradition with other denominations.

Everyone's daily life should be a balance of the "journey outward" and the "journey inward" — doing and being. But most people's lives are "do do" instead of "do be do be do," as the patron saint of freight train riders, Frank Sinatra of Hoboken, sang. In the Gnostic Gospel of Thomas, God is described as "a movement and a rest." We would do well to mimic our Maker.

▨ GLOSSARY ▨

Bad order – a train car with defects

Black hole – tunnel

Bull – railroad police; also cinder dicks, railroad dicks

Catching out – hopping a freight train

Caught the westbound – died

Cherry picker – machine used for pulling out railroad spikes

Cinder dick – railroad police; also bulls, railroad dicks

Date nail – nail put in railroad ties to indicate the year they were installed

Division point – town where trains change crews

Flashing rear end device (FRED) – device placed at the rear of a train in lieu of a caboose

Gandy dancer – laborer on a railroad track maintenance crew

Gay-cats – a 19th century term for a novice rail rider

Grainer – grain car

Helpers – extra engines added to get over a pass

Highballed – took off fast

Hobo – a hobo travels and works; a tramp travels and doesn't work; a bum doesn't travel or work

Hobo handle – nickname

Hobo jungle – place where hobos camp

Hobo mafia – allegedly the Freight Train Riders of America

Home guard – someone who has quit riding the rails

Hotbox – enclosure near the wheels that holds the train car's bearings

Hot yard – a yard with tough railroad police

Hot shot – a fast train with high priority

Hump – to jolt two railroad cars together; the continental divide; hill in yard used for building trains

In the hole – on a side track

Intermodal train – train carrying ship containers or highway truck trailers on flatcars

Joining the birds – jumping off a train

Low line – keep a low profile

Manifest train – train with a mix of freight cars (compare with unit train)

Midnight creeps – railroad cars that move quietly through a yard and can hit and kill you

Old Dirty Face – a freight train

On the cushions – riding a passenger train

On the fly – catching a train on the run

Piggybacks – highway truck trailers on specially built flatcars

Power transfer – train that is all engines

Railroad dicks – railroad police; also bulls, cinder dicks

Rails – railroad employees

Rat hole tunnel – one that fills with excessive fumes

Rattler – a freight train

Ride the rails – catch a freight train

Rolling stock – wheeled vehicles used by a railroad

Rolling the train – checking out a train to find a suitable place to ride

Ruling grade – steepest grade for a train

Section gang – a crew of track maintenance employees

Set off – dropping a railroad car off on a side track

Shortline railroads – smaller, local railroads

Slack action – occurs when a train starts, stops, or changes speed fast

Tag – cover with graffiti

Tokay blanket – drinking enough alcohol so you don't feel the cold

Two-tied it – my term for taking two ties per stride

Unit – engine

Unit train – train where all the railcars are the same (compare with manifest train)

Way car – what a caboose is sometimes called in the eastern portion of the U.S.

The Cruz family on vacation

As a family, it is perfectly safe to hop a freight train that cannot move, if the children are wearing their steel-toed flip-flops. It behooves the person in front to look back to make sure the rest of the crew fakes things properly — otherwise, one might get the impression that they are hopping a freight train that is not in motion.

Horses' asses determined the standard railroad gauge of 4 feet, 8-1/2 inches. The oldest existing track system was one created under Persian King Darius (who threw Daniel into the lion's den in the Old Testament story from the Bible). Darius created extensive military roads and grooves were cut into the surface of rock in the mountains to keep chariot wheels from sliding. The grooves were at the same centers as rails of standard gauge track today. The jigs and tools used to build chariots were later used to build wagons, then tramways and finally rail lines. Chariot wheel spacing was designed to accommodate the girth of the horses that pulled them. President Lincoln tried to get rail width changed to five feet but couldn't sway his bureaucrats. So horses' asses in government kept the old rail spacing. Moral: Just because you are a horse's ass now doesn't mean you can't get on track later.

Here are some other highlights from railroad history:

- In 1797, the steam locomotive was invented in England.
- In 1823, the first public railway in the world opened in England.
- In 1827, Baltimore merchants chartered the first railroad in North America – the Baltimore & Ohio (B&O) of *Monopoly* fame.
- In 1830, the first regular steam-powered rail passenger service in the U.S. began operation in South Carolina, utilizing the U.S.-built locomotive *The Best Friend of Charleston*. On June 17, 1831, the *Best Friend* became the first locomotive in the U.S. to suffer a boiler explosion. It was caused when the fireman tied down the steam pressure release valve because he got tired of listening to it whistle. (Our conscience is like that pressure relief valve. If we stop listening to it a karmic explosion is inevitable. When Saint Catherine of Siena was told that she made the Pope nervous, she said it was because she spoke to him out loud what his conscience told him in a whisper.)
- In 1833, Andrew Jackson became the first sitting president to ride the rails. Harry Truman was the last president to use railroads extensively.
- In 1833, a total of 380 miles of rail track were in operation in the U.S.; in 1840, about 2,800 miles; in 1850, more than 9,000 miles (as much as in the rest of the world combined); in 1860, over 30,000 miles.
- In 1860, President Abraham Lincoln formally inaugurated construction of the transcontinental railroad. It was completed in 1869 when the "Golden Spike" joined the Union Pacific and Central Pacific railroads at Promontory Point in Utah.
- From 1861 to 1865, the Civil War became the first major conflict in which railroads played a significant role.

- In 1865, the "Golden Age" of railroads began. For nearly half a century, no other mode of transportation challenged the railroads. The rail network grew from 35,000 to a peak of 254,000 miles in 1916.
- In the late 1800's, railroad workers noticed that empty freight cars made a different sound over track-joints than cars that were carrying a load. That "dead beat" meant the cars weren't paying their way. The term "deadbeat" came to encompass people who failed to carry their share of the load.
- In 1917, the federal government seized control of the railroads for the rest of World War I. They were returned in seriously run-down conditions.
- From 1900 to 1940, other subsidized modes of transportation (trucks, cars, etc.) challenged rail dominance.
- From 1929 to 1940, the Great Depression forced substantial segments of the railroad industry into bankruptcy.
- During World War II, railroads remained under private control.
- From 1945 to 1970, major railroad investment occurred and diesel engines replaced steam, but the decline in railroad market share continued.
- From 1970 to 1975, nine Class I railroads, almost one-quarter of the industry's trackage, filed for bankruptcy protection.
- The 1970, the Clean Air Act created demand for low-sulfur coal, leading to a western railroad revival. The Rail Passenger Service Act created Amtrak.
- In 1976, the Railroad Revitalization and Regulatory Reform Act created the Consolidated Rail Corporation (Conrail) from six bankrupt Northeast railroads.
- In 1980, the Stagger's Rail Act reduced the Interstate Commerce Commission's regulatory jurisdiction over railroads. That led to competition, advances in technology and a restructuring of the industry.
- In 1987, Conrail was privatized in the largest share offering in U.S. history. Investors paid nearly $2 billion to buy shares in the railroad.
- In 1996, the Interstate Commerce Commission was replaced by the Surface Transportation Board, which assumed responsibility for remaining railroad economic regulation.

🚂 APPENDIX B: LEVELS OF AWARENESS 🚂

In Chapter 25, I wrote, "I believe that all the major religions are like spokes on a wheel leading to the same hub (God). Each of the spiritual spokes has different levels of progression as it nears the hub – from the barbarian, to the fundamentalist, to the atheist, to the spiritual, to the mystic and finally, to oneness with the hub." The process wheel on the following page (figure 1) illustrates this concept. The chart was expanded and reconfigured from one in a Unity School of Christianity booklet called *Holy Spirit Regeneration*, which in turn was adapted from *The Incredible Journey* by Dr. Carol Ruth Knox.

The process wheel has five spokes leading from the outside rim to the hub. They represent the five major religions: Buddhism (B), Judaism (J), Islam (I), Christianity (C) and Hinduism (H). Of course, each major religion has many sects, not all of which will get you all the way back to God. Some non-major religions could get you to the center as well. I use these five for chart simplicity.

There are a series of five concentric circles of successively smaller circumference proceeding from the outer rim to the star at the center. These represent stages of spiritual awareness. On the outer rim is the "Barbarian/ Narcissistic" whose consciousness is barely above that of an animal. The second ring represents the "Religious/Conformist" phase. People at this level have low self-esteem; feel they have no control over life's events and believe in an anthropomorphic God. The third circle represents the "Atheistic/ Rational" stage. After a person rejects a fundamentalist perspective, they often go through this phase. (This is M. Scott Peck's idea from *The Road Less Traveled*.) The next ring is the "Spiritual/Synthesizing" level. In it, people develop more self-worth, believe that thoughts are things that can be controlled, and believe that they are co-creators along with God. The inner most circle is that of the "Mystic/Intuitive." Silent meditation with devotion is the primary tool used at this stage. The person becomes more selfless and surrenders to God rather than trying to co-create. God dangles material things before us to see what we want most — the gifts or the Giver. The mystic chooses the Giver. The star in the center represents the end of the journey, whereby people have realized their oneness with God again.

The inner rings represent higher levels of consciousness, but the people at these stages are not better than those at the outer levels — just as a person in third grade in school is no better than one in eleventh grade. Therefore, we shouldn't criticize anyone at a lower level. All levels are all fine as long as they are moving the person toward the Center (or preventing them from backsliding). If we stagnate at any particular level, life will nudge us forward — willingly or unwillingly.

LEVELS OF AWARENESS

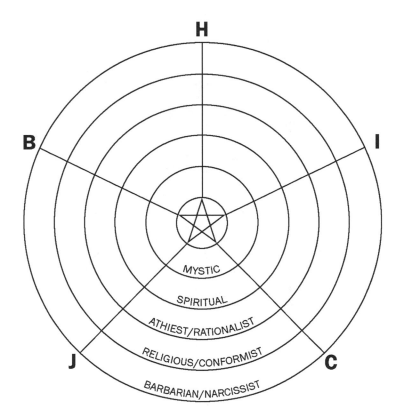

Figure 1

According to the intertwined theories of reincarnation and karma (that were wrongly eliminated from Christian teaching at the Second Council of Constantinople in 553 C. E.), we go through many lifetimes like grades in school with a period of vacation in between called death. We incarnate hundreds of times before we are through, sometimes in male bodies, sometimes in female bodies. Fortunately, we do not usually remember our past lives — the confusion would be unbearable. What we are today is the consequence of all of our actions in past lives. We are totally responsible for our current status.

Hindus visualize our individual existence as being like salt water encased in a corked bottle, that is encased in another corked bottle, that is encased in a third corked bottle, all floating on the ocean. The salt water in the inner bottle is our soul. The ocean is God. Both are made of the same salt water, but the bottle bodies separate them. The outer bottle is the physical body made up of electrons. The middle bottle is the body of energy or astral body made up of "lifetrons;" the innermost bottle is the body of ideas or casual body made up of "thoughtrons" (Paramahansa Yogananda coined these words). Each body bottle is stoppered with a cork of ignorance, which keeps us from knowing our true nature — oneness with God. Through many lifetimes we gradually pop the corks of ignorance and can then flow back into God.

As there are three bodies, so there are three worlds — the physical, the astral, and the causal. Physical death is astral birth. Astral death is physical birth. We rotate between the physical and astral worlds until we have no more physical desires. Then we rotate between the astral and the causal worlds until we have no more astral desires. When we have no more causal desires we are free — reunited with God once more, which is the sole purpose of life. Such a being is no longer compelled to reincarnate, but may do so at God's behest to help struggling humanity in their journey homeward. The founders of the major religions probably fit this category and are classified as "avatars." (Not the big blue humanoids from the film of the same name.)

Video cameras with zoom features help illustrate the difference between science and religion. If a camera is zoomed out and focused and then it is zoomed in, it goes out of focus and must be refocused. But if a camera is zoomed all the way in and is focused and then it zooms out, it always stays in focus. Science approaches knowledge from the outside in. As it gets more powerful tools and can zoom in closer, scientific theories go out of focus and must be refocused. "Avatars" are one with the Universe and proceed from the inside out. They have zoomed in and focused, so that whenever they zoom out, they are always in perfect focus. Their unchanging perspective must be given priority over science's ever-changing theories.

So scientific "facts" need to be closely scrutinized by spiritual giants, because the "facts" may well go out of focus in the future. Look at the humble egg. First science said it was good because it contained protein. Then science said it was bad because it was full of cholesterol. Now science says it is good again because much of that cholesterol is the "good" type. The egg never changed.

I came up with this next concept when I was a nineteen year-old sophomore at Yale in 1968 taking Religious Studies courses. It befuddles me a bit now, but it has proven helpful to others.

The graph of the function $xy = 1$ is called an asymptotic curve (figure 2). I will use it to help explore the relationship of science and religion. In this example, the y-axis is the time axis. As "y" becomes greater it represents a progression into historical time. The x-axis represents knowledge. As "x" approaches zero, humankind approaches ultimate knowledge (zero unknown). I define ultimate knowledge as God. The curve represents the prevailing knowledge that humankind had at their disposal at any point in historic time. This prevailing knowledge can be called "scientific knowledge" today. I put points on the curve to indicate the successive historical forms of community that have evolved over time: foraging, horticultural, agrarian, industrial, and informational. As humankind progresses in historic time, the curve approaches the ultimate knowledge y-axis, but will never reach it (since, to do so, "y" would have to be 0 and, in the function $xy = 1$, no "x" number multiplied by 0 can equal 1). The unknown area will always be infinite. No matter how much we discover there will always be an infinite amount that we do not know. That is the realm of Spirit.

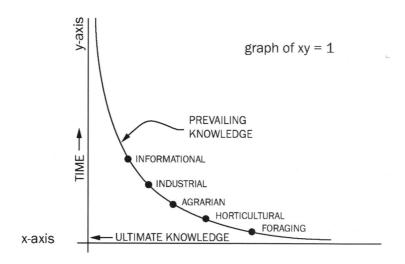

Figure 2

Science and Religion I

Humankind, in their desire to know God and attain ultimate knowledge, has tried to bridge the gap between what is known at any point in historic time and ultimate knowledge. The result is religion (figure 3). If an "avatar," a person who has already made it back to God (the y-axis), started that religion, it will endure and will have the tools to help others get back to God (religion A makes it to the y-axis). If a lesser mortal created it, it will disappear over time (religion B does not make it to the y-axis).

Prior to the scientific method (discovered in the late seventeenth century), religions had to sometimes provide answers to what were strictly scientific questions. If the religion's founders were avatars, they knew the scientific answers but couched them in allegory so people with the limited understanding of the time could grasp them to some degree. But the allegories were eventually interpreted literally. When the scientific method came into flower (period C on the graph), it disproved much of this literal base and seemingly undermined the religion. (The vertical dashed line from scientific period C intersects the religion A and B lines. The literal information to the right of that intersection — indicated by hash marks — seemingly becomes irrelevant). But if the literal information is once again interpreted allegorically, as was intended, the conflicts disappear to a large degree. So older religions, if founded by avatars, are still capable of making lurches forward when science has seemingly undercut some of their foundation. New religions with new answers based on new knowledge can also come into being (religion C).

Science needs to stay above the curve and religion needs to stay below it. Science oversteps its bounds when it makes metaphysical proclamations, like "life has no meaning." Religion needs to stop making up science that fits its literal interpretations and get allegorical.

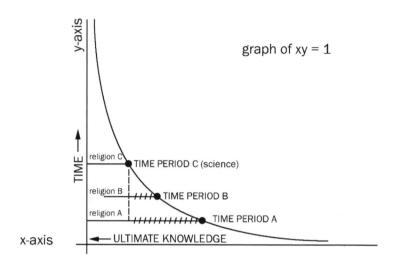

Figure 3

Science and Religion II

APPENDIX D:

🚂 THE BELL CURVE THEORY OF EVERYTHING 🚃

It seems to me that when we advance on the spiritual path (left to right in figure 4), we climb a material mountain made of desires and then, hopefully, descend again. The mountain is like a Bell curve. For example, at the foot of the mountain on the left side we are in *poverty*, at the peak we have *prosperity*, at the base of the mountain on the right side we achieve *simplicity*. Other triplets might be:

Left side	Mountain peak	Right side
Instinct	Intellect	Intuition
(body knowledge)	(mind knowledge)	(soul knowledge)
Low self-esteem	Healthy ego	No ego
Not doing	Doing	Being
Meat too costly	Meat eating	Vegetarianism
Sex repression	Sex expression	Sex transmutation
Doing what we want	Doing what we're taught	Doing what we ought
Tamas - a guna	Rajas - a guna	Sattva - a guna
(inertia/mass/obstruction)	(struggle/energy/activity)	(wisdom/intelligence/ expansion)

The hobo and the mystic are similar in many ways because both are at the base of the mountain but on opposite sides —

Hobo   Majority   Mystic

It seems like we all have to climb this mountain in order to have an adequate offering to give back to God. If we've made the climb over and over for many lifetimes, we hopefully learn to traverse to the other side and begin our descent sooner rather than later.

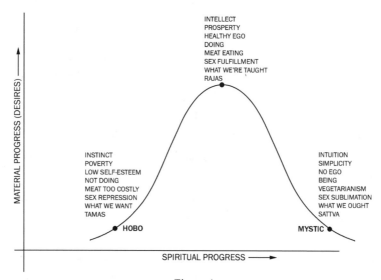

Figure 4

The Bell Curve Theory of Everything

About the cover artist: Erik C. Lindgren (www.erikclindgren.com)
Erik C. Lindgren paints with oil and other various mediums such as gouache, pastel, pencil, ink and acrylic. Most of his recent work is oil on canvas and has a driven obsession with detail and precision. Since his childhood growing up in the Midwest, he has developed a strong eye for details and the history behind his subjects. He has been an avid rail fan and automobile enthusiast since his childhood. A Magna Cum Laude graduate of Rocky Mountain College of Art & Design in Lakewood, Colorado, clients from around the world have utilized the award-winning skills of this photo-realist and fine artist. Erik and his wife Dawn reside in Arvada, Colorado.

About the photographer: Tom Lee (www.tomleephotographer.com)
Tom Lee is a fine art photographer who works with traditional black and white, silver-based film and paper. Using manual cameras, available light, and a simple darkroom, Tom's work explores the shadows, textures, shapes, and forms that make up the world. Nudes, urban landscapes, and still lifes are his primary subject matters. Tom's art can be found in many public and private collections throughout the United States. He has won numerous awards at regional and national competitions. Paralyzed by an automobile accident in 1974, Lee has adapted his cameras and darkroom facility. He operates his camera by biting down on a cable release to work the shutter. Tom and his wife Mary Katherine live in an old Catholic church in Norman, Oklahoma that they share with their many pets.

About the editor: Melynda Louise Saldenais
(www.melyndasaldenais.com)
Melynda is a writer, editor, food stylist, recipe developer and culinary video producer who is passionate about anything related to food, travel and spiritual enlightenment. Her two companies, Melynda Louise Saldenais, LLC and Melynda's Kitchen, LLC provide creative solutions for writing, editing, marketing and video needs, in both the food realm and for natural, organic and green lifestyles. She tells verbal and visual stories in a meaningful and impactful manner, and she is as adept with a noun or a verb as she is with a spatula and saucier.

About the Cruz family: Sue, Bill, Asia, and Elena
They created the whimsical photo and caption that appears just before the appendix section. They live in Wisconsin.

Photo by Tom Lee

Born in Wisconsin, raised in Minnesota, Wayne was the doubtless All-American boy — high school class president, A-student, accidental All-American in football. Destiny's course took him to Yale University, but he had an identity crisis and, *Wiffenpoof*, [1] he was gone. He started to roam and hop freight trains. Wayne fully recovered from his Yale experiences and eventually graduated from The Evergreen State College in Olympia, Washington with a degree in Environmental Studies and Land Use Planning. He became a city planner in western ski areas, and then went monastic for seven years to find the best environment in which to meditate. Marriage to a terrific woman has settled him down — a bit. Wayne has been dividing his time between Alaska, Colorado, and Oklahoma for the last two years, while his wife lovingly keeps the home fires burning. They plan to move back to Colorado soon.

The author's qualifications to write this book are obvious from the text itself — twelve years of extensive rail riding and seven years as a monk. He has won two writing contests: 1) a *Why I Like Wyatt Earp* contest in grade school (he broke his prize — plastic Buntline Special revolvers — in two days); and 2) third place in a *Park City E.A.R.* writing contest with a hobo story. A hobo and a children's story were produced for community radio in

---

1 The *Yale Wiffenpoofs* are the oldest collegiate *a cappella* group in the United States, established in 1909.

Aspen, Colorado. A comedy called *Tenitis* was produced for the *Five-Minute Play Festival* in Aspen. A non-satirical parody of Father Thomas Keating's incredible work called *Night of Sense of Humor* was performed in Denver for his national faculty and in Boston for a Contemplative Outreach national convention. *Chasing Messiahs*, a stage play, was given a glorified staged reading in Aspen and later converted into a screenplay. Wayne has developed a detailed step outline and back-stories for either a television series or trilogy of films based on *Hobo Sapien*. He is working on a stage play called *Wanda Wakes* that gives a hobo perspective from the point of view of a wife who was left behind. A book of non-freight train hopping adventures is also in the works.

Wayne is also an entertaining speaker, having given numerous talks, sermons, and workshops in Utah, Colorado, Oklahoma, and Texas, and natural history tours in Alaska. He will be available as a speaker after his next stint at Denali National Park in Alaska is over in late September 2010. Contact Wayne at www.wisehobo.com.

STUDENT COMMENTS

In the fall of 2009, Professor Tom Boyd of the University of Oklahoma used *Hobo Sapien* as a text in his Religious Studies class titled "Religion, Culture, and the Meaning of Life." He stated:

In a class of fifty-eight students virtually all of them, with only half a dozen exceptions, were complimentary of the use of the text. They especially liked two features. First, a wide range of comments indicated having learned much about hobo life and the history of the railroads in the western United States. Second, many students found the spiritual insights and the lessons at the end of the chapters especially compelling. In fact, some students stated that they wish this aspect of the book had been expanded. In general students noted that they appreciated being exposed to the life of a person who had lived such a distinctive life.

Mr. Iverson spoke to the class and students took a substantial reading test on the text. Grades were especially strong, indicating that students had read the text with care. All in all, the assignment and student responses suggested that the use of the book was helpful to their learning.

Students were given extra credit on the test for writing a statement evaluating the book and its worth to them as a reader. Their reviews were turned over to the author, but their names were not provided. A selection of their comments is listed below.

1. I believe *Hobo Sapien* was an easy, entertaining read with insight on a way of life very unknown to me. The metaphors between real life and spirituality were often quite clever and made a complicated subject easier to understand.
2. This book was an incredibly interesting one. The way that he tied the spiritual meanings into his biography was unique. It didn't come off as either too biographical or repetitively spiritual.
3. Iverson's book is a smooth read and does a great job mixing its autobiographical, spiritual, and historical elements. The lesson at the end of each of the short chapters makes it feel like a devotional, and he might want to market it that way…. Again its short, concise chapters and compelling bits of history and life are its best aspects in its current form.
4. *Hobo Sapien* was a good book to read. It was very entertaining overall, a book you usually don't see or read often. It taught me many things about religion and life as I was going through them while reading the book. Phrases such as "Life is a parade; find your float" stuck with me because not everyone has the same viewpoint. We find what brings us happiness and join in with everyone else living life.

5. I had never met a hobo before you came and spoke to our class. You really exceeded my expectation. What even further surprised me was that while most people had either book smarts or street smarts, you had both kinds. Kudos to you. The parts in your book that were most insightful were the parts about intuition and science.... You have not only broken my expectations about hobos, but also helped to surpass my current awareness of my religious and spiritual self. Very nicely done.

6. I really enjoyed reading Iverson's book *Hobo Sapien*. I have never read about or been educated on the life of a hobo, thus I found it very interesting. Many of his ideas about spirituality throughout the book were very similar to my beliefs. I also enjoyed reading the stories that happen in and around Oklahoma. I think it gave help to some people's understanding about Oklahoma and Texas history. Overall the book was great with good quotes about his beliefs on life and God.

7. The book was extremely well written. I found myself immersed in the stories and the history of the railroads. I even told my friends some of the stories in your book because I was so amazed by them.... Overall, I really enjoyed *Hobo Sapien*.

8. This book was truly an awesome read and I would recommend it to anyone in a heartbeat. I found myself reading faster than usual and I would look down at the page number and I was further than expected. I laughed at the witticisms at the end of the chapters, wrote down some of the Godly advice, and didn't want to put the book down. I have already inserted some of the knowledge I have gained into daily conversations and thoroughly enjoyed this read. Definitely my kind of book.

9. I enjoyed the way *Hobo Sapien* was written, concise and simple. The ways in which the experience and spirituality were linked was wonderful.

10. Throughout this book there were things I agreed with and highlighted to remember. There were things I disagreed with that were recorded for future thought and reflection. Overall, I thought I was learning from an old friend who proved to me that my journey could be made more bright although more challenging.

11. *Hobo Sapien* was an illuminating view on life I had never been exposed to previously. The language and style is raw but the truth stated by the author is profound and raised great discussion in my own life. Any book that makes me stop reading it to stop and think has value.

12. The book sheds light on the many ways rigidity can be broken on our spiritual journey. Being confined to one way of thinking only confines our approach to unlocking spiritual truths. That message is one of ultimate worth to me as a reader.

13. ... I very much like the title; it is interesting and an accurate description of the book. But overall, I value the contents in this story. It was thought provoking and entertaining. I don't believe Iverson wants us to see it as a guide to live our lives but a resource to use to advance and open our minds on our mystical path. Even while studying the text some

classmates and I would stop and go into discussion over the material. We sometimes would even call up family members [and] friends to ask their opinions because of something that was presented in such a unique method.... I believe Iverson would like knowing his views and stories broadened our own views on our spiritual lives since that is what getting closer to the center of the wheel is all about. This is definitely a text I would recommend for others to read. It was an easy read with a deep meaning and profound thoughts. I enjoyed how honest it was and the uniqueness of the story.

14. You're not seeking meaning in the small things of life if you can't relate to Iverson's book, *Hobo Sapien*. His stories were extremely entertaining, often provoking audible responses, from a seemingly easy read. It was far more than surface. Iverson has a knack for siphoning meaning and truth from his uncommon life and if there is one thing about truth, it's relatable. I had a great time reading it and have enjoyed extending the power of the word "hobo" into more than just a noun.

15. Hobo Sapien challenged me in many ways. The railroad stories provided great parables so I could grasp the concepts. Also the biggest challenge the book gave me was to daily meditate so that I can grow spiritually. Also the book's idea that we sin but aren't sinners shook me up. It made me feel like life has a purpose and all is not lost when we sin. Not only did the book challenge me, it gave me many good laughs!

16. As an individual who feels lost in their spiritual adventure, this opened my eyes, mind, and heart to ways to achieve the oneness with God I have been longing for.

17. As a student, it's easy to get annoyed when receiving an assigned reading. After the first few chapters, however, I was pleasantly surprised at how easy it was to become engulfed in his stories. Excellent book! Definitely a page-turner!

18. The book, *Hobo Sapien*, caused me to dig deep into my beliefs and challenged me on many of them. A lot of Iverson's beliefs I feel I also share, but have almost been too scared to experience or meditate on due to the traditions and beliefs I was raised on. Though I'm not positive what exactly changed, this book has caused me to think and reevaluate my own beliefs and actions. Iverson's writing was very understandable and his humor and personality were very relatable.

19. This book was extremely enjoyable and readable. The final paragraph of each chapter reveals true spiritual wisdom that is worth remembering. Furthermore, I was surprised by how much I learned about the railroad, and how much respect I gained for the hobo.

20. Hobo Sapien by Wayne Iverson was a very moving book. It will inspire audiences everywhere with its bittersweet morality.... Overall, the book was a great read. I will definitely be purchasing a copy for my sister when it is published!

21. *Hobo Sapien* was truly enlightening. Iverson gave a refreshing perspective to the ideals of religion without preaching some sort of religious testament. His parables were unique and fun to read, and the morals presented at the end of each chapter brought the stories to an interesting and understandable full circle.

22. *Hobo Sapien* was one of, if not the most, interesting books I've read. It comes from an experience and opinion that almost every American has not experienced or acknowledged, and therefore possesses an interesting power to shift and change world-views of the reader. I think that each story is captivating and humorous and the spiritual truths tied into the ending are respectfully given and easily understood. I thoroughly enjoyed reading *Hobo Sapien*.

23. At first Iverson's approach to unfolding his experiences confused me, but as his stories and conclusions began to map out his religious outlook, I realized they chronicled his journey in the way of a hobo. Free-spirited. Unfettered. Unconventional. But exciting! His lessons were interesting and I enjoyed learning about how he came to his conclusions.

24. I really enjoyed *Hobo Sapien* because it was an easy read and very entertaining. I liked the construction of the book because it always had a little something to take from the end of each chapter. Iverson does well in describing his adventures and informing the reader when informing was needed and when it was not. As the reader, I pulled many good lessons from the book that I will try to incorporate into my own life. While I do not plan on *catching out* anytime soon, I will definitely cherish the ideas and arguments Iverson puts forth in this exciting book.

25. I'm not a very religious person because I can't relate to the stories I usually hear. These stories are more my style of relating to religion. They are believable and I can relate to the life lessons at the end of the stories. They make sense and are very reasonable. The lessons at the end are simple but can mean so much to an enormous amount of different people.

26. I liked the book because he showed how all his experiences helped him progress on his religious path. He is also very open-minded and does not try to convince the reader to believe the same way he does.

27. Iverson's book challenged me to look deeper in everyday life in order to see how God moves simply and effortlessly through it. It was a fun read with raw and simple insight. It's even making me consider meditation.

28. I found *Hobo Sapien* interesting, easy to read, and enlightening. The author was very clear about what he was trying to convey, and I was never bored while reading this text.

29. I really liked this book. I enjoyed his words of wisdom and many of the quotes he incorporated. I actually wrote some of them down I liked them so much…. I loved his stories, especially the one about the shoelaces and how he related it to understanding suffering. I read that part to my roommate. She is going through a very bad break [up and it helped her] make sense of things.

30. I found this book very enlightening and upbeat. He found a new way to teach me the lessons I had learned before, but never really knew how to apply them spiritually. His sense of humor was very refreshing as well.

31. Being a person that thoroughly enjoys structure in my life, I found it hard to grasp onto the hobo way of mind. However after a few pages in, I fell in love with this book; I believe we share the same sense of humor. My favorite part about it was the sheer honesty put into it. It was raw and unique…. I loved the insights of wisdom, or lack thereof, at the end of the chapters. This book was exactly what I needed at this time in my life! I have already been telling people about it! This book has real down to earth insight. I feel many types of people could gain a lot from reading this easy read! … All the pros out weigh the cons, and I know I will be reading *Hobo Sapien* many more times!

32. The book had a great story and history, but the religious paragraphs at the end of each chapter were remarkable. I felt like I was reading a fortune cookie of information on what God does for us and how he doesn't cause bad things upon us but we put them on ourselves and we control our lives with God's helpful push.

33. Hobo Sapien was a very informative, interesting, mind-boggling text. Iverson presented his writing in a very non-traditional way, which I thoroughly enjoyed and kept me interested [and] intrigued. His parables suited his stories well. From [word cut off] in his non-traditional viewpoints with strong God-oriented lessons, he shook my beliefs. I would be right on key with his stories, and then he would have a "moral" attaching [it] to God. I'm not much of a believer, but he made all of the coincidences I have pondered seem like the work of God's omnipresence…. The science vs. religion appendix was very difficult to fully comprehend, however, it literally blew my [mind].

34. I thought *Hobo Sapien* was a compelling story. I really enjoyed how at the end of each chapter he would go back and make it almost into a parable but at the same time stress every story doesn't have to have a moral. While reading the story I found myself relating his journey, struggles, and achievements to my own.

35. I thought that it provided a much-needed knowledge and enlightened me in many of the statements. It made me think about things that I would have never thought about before.

36. When I was reading the book I always looked forward to the end of the chapters to hear the lesson about God. I also enjoyed the jokes. Yesterday when I was studying for this test I was having a horrible day and reading over the lessons at the end of the chapters helped me out a lot. They are very interesting to read and very inspiring.

Stay on track.